THE ACTION STORYBOOK BIBLE

An Interactive Adventure through
God's Redemptive Story

ILLUSTRATIONS BY SERGIO CARIELLO

TEXT BY CATHERINE DEVRIES

David C Cook®
transforming lives together
www.davidccook.com

THE ACTION STORYBOOK BIBLE
Published by David C Cook
4050 Lee Vance Drive
Colorado Springs, CO 80918 U.S.A.

David C Cook U.K., Kingsway Communications
Eastbourne, East Sussex BN23 6NT, England

The graphic circle C logo is a registered
trademark of David C Cook.

LCCN 2017933740

ISBN 978-0-7814-1420-3

eISBN 978-1-4347-1146-5

Text © 2017 David C Cook

Illustrations © 2017 Sergio Cariello Studio, Inc.

The Team: Catherine DeVries, Amy Konyndyk, Ashley Ward,
Stephanie Bennett, Leigh Davidson, Susan Murdock

Cover Design: Amy Konyndyk

Printed in the United States of America

First Edition 2017

1 2 3 4 5 6 7 8 9 10

062817

Presented To:

_____

From:

_____

Date:

_____

CONTENTS

NEW TESTAMENT

Greetings, fellow *Action Bible* fans!

I just wanted to write to let you know how excited I am for the newest—and youngest—addition to *The Action Bible*® collection … *The Action Storybook Bible*! For this new book, I have drawn brand-new pictures to reach families with kids ages eight and under so that together, you can explore stories from the Bible. The pictures took me two years to draw! They will guide you from scene to scene, building up through each story episode. (When you reach the end of each one, talk about the questions with your family.) You'll see the art style has my "hand print" on it and what you expect from all things Action Bible—packed with plenty of action and drama—but it's a little simpler and easier to follow. I pray that God may use this book to impact your life, not only telling you about God's amazing stories but also encouraging you in your journey

  as a son or daughter of the almighty God. I pray this book helps you put your faith into action so you may be a light to this dark world so desperately in need of a Savior.

As a storyteller, I want to not only *show* the words on the page but also *tell* God's stories so you feel as if you are there in the moment, hearing them unfold. While I was writing this book, I read each story out loud, often to my own family. I also enlisted their help with the "sound effects" throughout the book. Thanks to Bryce, Breia, Brent, and especially their dad and my husband, Brad. Their leading through the Holy Spirit was so important to this project.

 Readers and fellow storytellers, may this mixture of words and pictures inspire your family to take this adventure through God's redemptive story! God has been—and always will be—at work in the lives of His people. I can't wait to see how He will use this book to work in yours.

Catherine DeVries

GOD CREATES THE WORLD

Based on Genesis 1—3

In the beginning there was nothing but God. He had a plan. God said, "Let there be light," and there was light. The light was good. God split the light from the darkness. That was the first day.

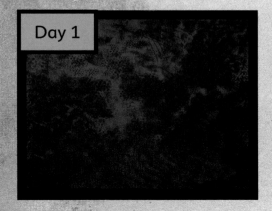

Day 1

Day 2

Then God separated the waters above from the waters below. He called the waters above "sky," and the waters below He called "oceans." That was the second day.

Day 3

Then God made room for dry land. He called it "earth," and it was good. Then God made plants and trees with seeds and fruit. That was the third day.

Day 4

God filled the skies with the sun, moon, and stars to separate daytime from nighttime. And so there was evening and morning—the fourth day.

Day 5

On the fifth day, God filled the seas with ocean creatures and filled the sky with birds … flipping, diving, swooshing, and gliding.

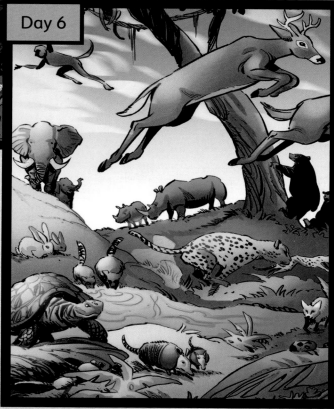

Day 6

And then beginning on the sixth day, God filled the earth with living creatures … creeping, crawling, running, jumping, and leaping!

Also on the sixth day, God made a man in His image. And from the man's rib, God made a woman. The man's name was Adam. The woman's name was Eve. They were made for each other and God blessed them. He put them in charge of the earth and everything in it. God told them to take good care of everything God had made. God saw all that He had made and said, "It is good, very good."

Day 7

Then God rested on the seventh day and made it holy. And so by His marvelous hand, God created the light and darkness; the oceans and sky; the land, plants, and animals; and human beings—all of creation.

Adam and Eve lived in a place called the garden of Eden. It had trees like a park and animals like a zoo, but there were no fences or cages because all the animals got along.

"Hello, there," came a sudden greeting from a serpent in the Tree of the Knowledge of Good and Evil. The serpent slithered close to Eve.

Eve was surprised by the serpent. She said, "You are in the forbidden tree."

"Oh, I love this tree," the serpent said. "Its fruit makes you know what God knows. It makes you powerful, just like God. And it's so delicious-sss."

"But ..." Eve hesitated, "God told us not to eat the fruit from this tree."

"Why not decide for your-ssself what you will and won't do?"

The fruit looked so good to Eve. She became confused. The rule God had given her and Adam didn't make sense now. She kept thinking about the serpent's words. She kept thinking about how delicious the fruit would taste ...

Eve made her decision. Her teeth crunched into the fruit, and it tasted delicious. She had to tell Adam!

"Oh, Adam, there you are!" Eve said. "I was just talking to a serpent. Now I will be like God since I ate this fruit. And you can be too. Take a bite! It's so delicious!"

"But isn't it from the Tree of the Knowledge of Good and Evil?" Adam hesitated. "You know God told us not to eat the fruit from that tree. But it does look delicious ..."

Adam couldn't resist. He ate the fruit too. It was every bit as delicious as promised. But then suddenly everything changed. Adam and Eve realized they were naked. They made clothes from fig leaves. And instead of wanting to talk with God, they hid from Him.

"Where are you?" God asked. "Why are you hiding from me? What have you done? Did you eat from the tree that I told you not to?"

"Yes," Adam admitted, "but Eve made me do it."

Then Eve said, "The serpent made me do it."

"Cursed be the serpent," God said. "Now, Adam and Eve, you must go. You must leave the garden of Eden because you disobeyed me. Your life will be hard. But I will still be with you."

Life, Faith, Action!

GOD IN ACTION

What a beautiful world God made—from the tiny ant to the huge blue whale, from delicate flowers to towering trees. We know that God also created people. No one is the same, not even twins! Our hair is different, and our eyes are different. Some of us are short, and others are tall. Our fingerprints are unique. God has a specific purpose for you, and He loves you exactly the way you are.

FAITH IN ACTION

Think of ways your family can appreciate God's creation together. Take a walk outside and talk about your favorite things in nature. Or cook a meal together using fresh fruits and vegetables and discuss where they came from.

Dear God, our Creator, thank you for making this beautiful world and all the wonderful plants and animals. And thank you for making each of us unique. Help us appreciate everything and everyone you've created, as well as do our part to take care of the world and one another. Amen.

PEOPLE FALL DEEP INTO SIN

Based on Genesis 4—9

After Adam and Eve had to leave the garden of Eden, life became much, much harder. There was more work to do because people had to plant and gather their own food. And having children was painful too. There weren't hospitals or doctors yet who could help.

Adam and Eve had three children. But sin tore the family apart. One brother named Cain killed another brother named Abel— all because Cain was jealous of Abel and his good relationship with God. Cain ran away. After that, Adam and Eve's third son, Seth, was born.

What would become of this world God created? It was just getting more and more evil … God saw all the sin everywhere and He was sorry He had made the world.

Families grew and spread out across the land. Soon almost everyone had forgotten about God.

But there was one man who was still faithful to God. His name was Noah. He and his wife had three sons—Shem, Ham, and Japheth.

God told Noah to do something that didn't make sense. Do you know what it was? God told Noah to build a boat. Not just a small boat for his family but a massive boat that would also fit …

… animals! Two of every kind—one male and one female. For the animals used for food, they were to bring seven pairs, and also seven pairs of birds.

Noah didn't understand, but he did what God told him to do.

If Noah didn't understand, can you imagine what everyone else thought? They made fun of Noah all the time.

This was the biggest project Noah had ever worked on. It took years and years, even decades! But Noah kept at it. He worked very hard. One day as he was finally finishing, Noah looked up, and there before him were animals as far as the eye could see.

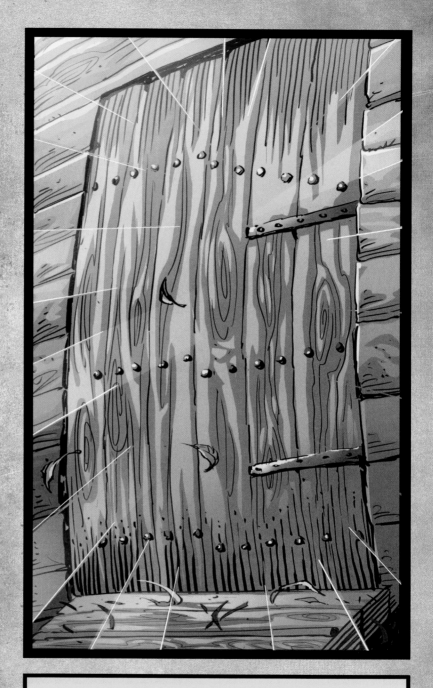

Noah wasted no time. He and his family loaded up the animals and supplies. Then God shut the door.

It rained and rained and rained. Days turned into weeks. It rained forty days and forty nights.

KABOOM

Nothing survived—except for the ark and everything inside it. Because of all the rain, the water rose higher and higher, covering the entire world. Noah and his family couldn't even see the tops of any mountains.

After a while, life in the ark settled into a daily routine for Noah, his wife, their three sons, and their sons' wives. They worked and waited and watched.

Living on the ark was like living on a floating zoo. Everyone had plenty of work to do. Noah's family all helped. None of them knew how long they would be on the boat, so all they could do was wait. They were in the ark for one full year!

Noah sent out a raven to see if it could find land. But the bird came back. Then Noah sent out a dove, but it also came back. A week later, Noah tried again. The dove flew back with an olive branch in its beak! Noah waited another week and sent out the dove again. It did not return. This was the sign Noah had been waiting for!

The ark came to rest on top of Mount Ararat (now in the country of Turkey). Gradually the water went down, lower and lower, until Noah and his family could see land all around.

God opened the door. All of God's creatures, along with Noah and his family, came out of the ark.

God placed a rainbow in the sky. It was a sign of His promise to never use a flood to destroy the earth again.

Noah and his family praised God. They built an altar and thanked God for saving them and for giving the world a fresh start.

Life, Faith, Action!

GOD HATES SIN

GOD IN ACTION

God sent the flood to wipe away all the sin in the world. But sin crept back and began pulling people away from God and all the good things He has for us. The rainbow is God's promise to never use a flood to destroy the world again. It is a great comfort to us, especially when we see rainbows after storms. Yes, God hates sin, but He loves us so much that He made the way to wipe out sin once and for all, so we can go to heaven to live with Him someday.

Want to know more about this? Go to page 225!

FAITH IN ACTION

Talk about rainbows together. When was the last time you saw one? When do they appear? Why are they a sign of hope? As a family, draw a rainbow and put it on your refrigerator as a reminder of God's promise.

God, thank you for your love for us. Please help us turn away from sin and instead live in ways that honor you. When we are tempted, help us encourage one another to resist and be strong! Amen.

GOD'S COVENANT PROMISE

Based on Genesis 15, 17—18, 20—22

On a quiet night, a man was gazing at the stars in the sky. Suddenly God called his name: "Abram!" God had something very important to tell him.

Abram believed in God. And even though Abram was afraid, he was ready to listen.

God said, "I will make you into a great nation. You will have as many children as the stars you see in the sky tonight. This is my promise, a covenant I am making between you and me."

"But how can this be?" Abram asked. "I don't have even one child, let alone a sky full of them!"

Abram told his wife, Sarai, that God had promised they would be parents. They waited many, many years. In fact, they waited so long that they got old. God spoke to Abram again, and changed their names to Abraham (which means "father of a multitude") and Sarah (which means "princess").

One day three visitors appeared and told them God's promise would still come true. Abraham rushed around, gathering up the best food he had, and he and Sarah prepared a nice meal for their unexpected guests.

When Sarah overheard the visitors tell Abraham that she would
have a baby, she laughed. "I am an old woman now," Sarah
said. "After all my young years have gone by, how can this
happen to me now?"

They all heard her laugh, but she denied it because she was
scared she would get into trouble.

Even though she had laughed about it, Sarah did become pregnant, and about one year later she gave birth to a precious baby boy. Abraham and Sarah named him Isaac, which means "he laughs."

Isaac grew older, and so did Abraham and Sarah. They kept trusting in God's plan.

God tested Abraham's trust. It was a very hard test—the hardest one Abraham would ever face.

"Take your son, your one and only son, to the top of the mountain," God said. "Sacrifice him there on an altar."

Abraham couldn't believe what he was hearing. He didn't understand. But he packed the supplies for the trip. He took two servants and a donkey with him, and he and Isaac headed up the mountain.

They went higher and higher.

Abraham felt confused, and his heart was heavy. The wood for the offering clattered on the donkey's back. The trail was rough, and the sun was hot. Isaac probably sensed that something just didn't feel right.

When they finally got to the top of the mountain, Abraham began unpacking the wood and setting up the altar.

"I see the wood," Isaac said, "but where is the sacrifice?"

Abraham replied, "God will provide the sacrifice."

Can you imagine how Abraham must have felt? But he still kept getting the altar ready, and he kept trusting in God.

Isaac lay down on the altar, and Abraham reached for his knife. He knew he had to obey God above everything else, even above his own will.

Just in time, God sent an angel of the Lord who said, "Stop! Abraham, I know now that you won't hold back your son—the one I had promised you for so many years."

What a huge relief Abraham and Isaac felt when they saw a bush nearby. There, with its horns stuck in the branches, was a ram. The ram would be the sacrifice!

God was very pleased with Abraham because he had passed the test.

God told Abraham, "Because you have shown me you are faithful, this covenant that I make with you shall be for all time. I will be your God, and you will be my people. I will make you into a great, great nation."

When Isaac was older, he married Rebekah, and they had many children. And his children had many children.

Soon God's people had indeed grown into a great nation. God had big plans for His people.

God kept His promises. Would His people be able to keep their part of the covenant with God?

Life, Faith, Action!

GOD KEEPS HIS PROMISES

GOD IN ACTION

Abraham and Sarah waited a long time before God's promise of a son came true. They learned to trust God, and they learned to wait for His timing. Even though it was so hard to wait, it was worth it because God's promise was bigger than they could have ever imagined. This promise began God's very important relationship, His covenant, with His people. Through good times and bad, God was always with His people, just as He had promised. And He is still with us today.

FAITH IN ACTION

As a family, talk about when you had to wait a very long time for something. What was hard? What were some things you learned from the experience? How did you see God at work?

Dear God, you know what is best for us, including the exact timing for when your promises come true. Help us to be patient. Help us to trust in your plan for our lives and your perfect timing. Amen.

FROM FAVORITE TO FORGOTTEN ... TO FAVORITE

Based on Genesis 37, 39—46

Remember Abraham? God made a covenant (a promise) with him and all his family who came after him—that He would be their God and they would be His people. One of those relatives was Abraham's grandson named Jacob.

Jacob had many sons, twelve in all! He made something very special for one of them ... Can you guess which son he gave it to?

Was it the oldest son, Reuben? Was it the youngest son, Benjamin?

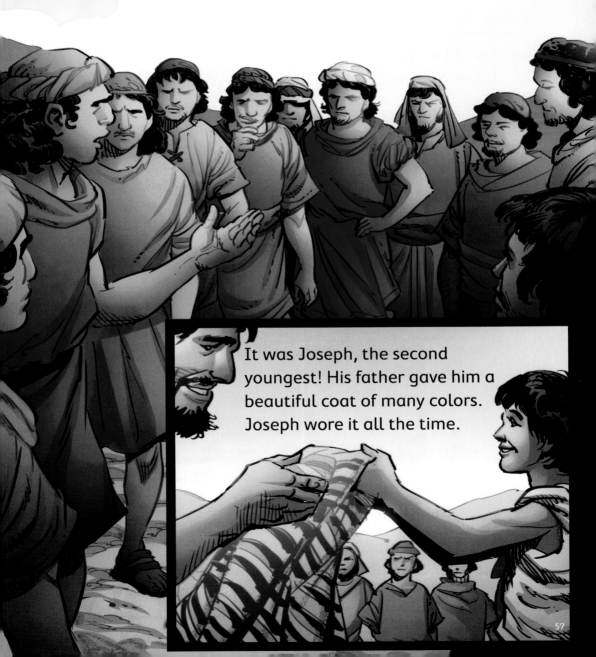

It was Joseph, the second youngest! His father gave him a beautiful coat of many colors. Joseph wore it all the time.

Yes, Joseph was the favorite son. There was no doubt about it.

Joseph's brothers were jealous. In fact, their anger burned against him. They couldn't stand him. Joseph told them that someday they would bow down to him. *Nothing could be further from the truth*, they all thought. There was no way they would ever do that!

One day Joseph was out in the field watching over the family's flock of sheep, and his brothers decided to put an end to him.

They ripped his beautiful coat from him. And then they threw him down into a deep pit.

Joseph's brothers decided to sell Joseph as a slave rather than leave him to die in the pit. Traders were traveling through the area on their way to Egypt.

The brothers waved down the traders, and the men paid twenty shekels (about 160 dollars) for Joseph. The traders took Joseph away to Egypt.

And Joseph's brothers thought that was the last time they would ever see him.

The brothers tore Joseph's robe and put blood on it, so it looked like a wild animal had attacked Joseph. They brought the torn and bloody coat to their father. And his heart was broken.

Meanwhile, Joseph and the traders had arrived in Egypt. And Joseph was offered up for sale again.

A man named Potiphar bought Joseph. Potiphar was an important official who worked for Pharaoh (who ruled over Egypt like a king).

God was with Joseph, and he did an outstanding job at every task Potiphar gave him. So Potiphar gave Joseph more and more to do.

Soon Joseph was in charge of Potiphar's household and everything Potiphar owned!

Potiphar's wife thought Joseph was handsome, and she wanted him to spend time with her alone—just the two of them.

Joseph knew this meant trouble and he wanted to get away. So he ran out of the house. He wanted nothing to do with her.

This made Potiphar's wife mad, and she lied about Joseph to her husband. She twisted the truth to make Joseph look like the bad guy.

Potiphar believed his wife and threw Joseph in jail. But God remembered Joseph … again. Even in jail, Joseph kept his faith in the Lord. Everyone who knew Joseph could easily see that he was extremely talented and blessed by God.

Prisoners came and went. But Joseph stayed in prison for a long time—for years.

Then one day Pharaoh's baker and his cupbearer were also thrown in jail.

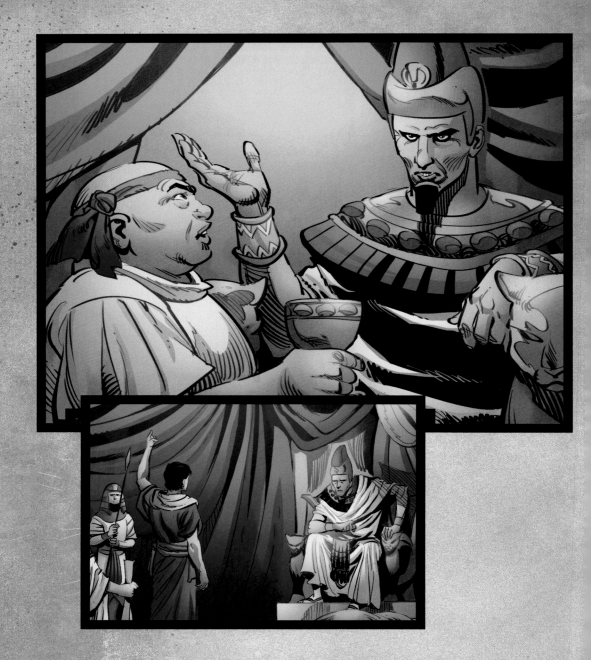

Even though it took a long, long time, eventually the cupbearer got out of jail and worked for Pharaoh again. He told Pharaoh about Joseph, and Joseph got out of jail too.

Joseph helped Pharaoh prepare for a famine that was coming, when there wouldn't be enough food in the land. God had told Joseph about this in a dream.

Sure enough, the famine came as Joseph had predicted. It spread to all the land—even to Joseph's family. His brothers traveled to Egypt in search of food.

They didn't recognize Joseph, but he recognized them.
    Finally Joseph burst out with the news that he was their brother … and can you guess what happened? His brothers bowed down to Joseph, just like he said they would long ago! Soon the rest of Joseph's family moved to Egypt. When Joseph's father saw him, his heart broke again—with joy!

Life, Faith, Action!

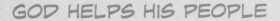

GOD IN ACTION

God was with Joseph every moment of his life. Joseph lost his family and then his freedom, first when he was sold as a slave and then when he was put in jail. But over and over again, God remembered Joseph and helped him succeed. God not only helps improve our situations, He also helps strengthen our hearts. For Joseph that meant God changed his heart so he could forgive his brothers.

FAITH IN ACTION

Talk about a hard time you have experienced as a family. How did you help one another? How did God help? Did it involve forgiving someone? Perhaps someone in your own family?

Dear God, we know that you care about everything that happens to us. May we remember that even when we face hard times, we are never alone. We have one another as a family and, most of all, we have you as our amazing God to help us in every moment. Thank you for always being with us. Amen.

THE GREAT RESCUE

Based on Exodus 2—20

Many years after Joseph, God's people became slaves to the pharaoh in Egypt. But still, God's people increased in number. In fact, Pharaoh thought there were too many of them. So he ordered that every baby boy born to a slave be killed.

Moses' mother knew her baby was in danger. But she had a plan.

She made a floating basket for Moses, and she told his sister, Miriam, to tuck him inside and set the basket in the reeds along the river to hide him. Then Miriam watched over him.

Miriam spotted some women near the water ... and one of them was a princess!

"Oh! What do we have here?" the princess wondered. She asked a servant to get the basket, and there was baby Moses, cooing and smiling at her.

The princess decided to adopt baby Moses, and so he grew up as a prince in Pharaoh's palace!

As Moses got older, he couldn't stand the way God's people were being treated. They were still slaves under the rule of Pharaoh. Moses got angry one day and killed one of the slave masters. He knew he had to escape from Egypt right away.

Moses rushed away to the countryside. He got married and became a shepherd. One day he saw a bush on fire, but it wasn't burning up. God spoke from this bush. He told Moses to rescue God's people, who were still slaves in Egypt. Moses didn't want to go back, but God insisted.

"Who shall I say sent me?" Moses asked.
   "I AM who I AM," God said.

When Moses went back to Egypt to see Pharaoh, Moses' brother Aaron joined him. They told Pharaoh to let God's people go.

But Pharaoh said, "No!" Even after bad things (called plagues) started to happen, Pharaoh still said no, over and over again, until God sent the last plague ... that took the life of Pharaoh's own son.

GO!

"Go! Get out of here. Take the slaves with you!" Pharaoh screamed, filled with grief and rage.

So Moses and God's people left Egypt.

But it didn't take long before Pharaoh changed his mind.

"After them, after them!" he ordered his army.

God's people were trapped next to the Red Sea with no way out.

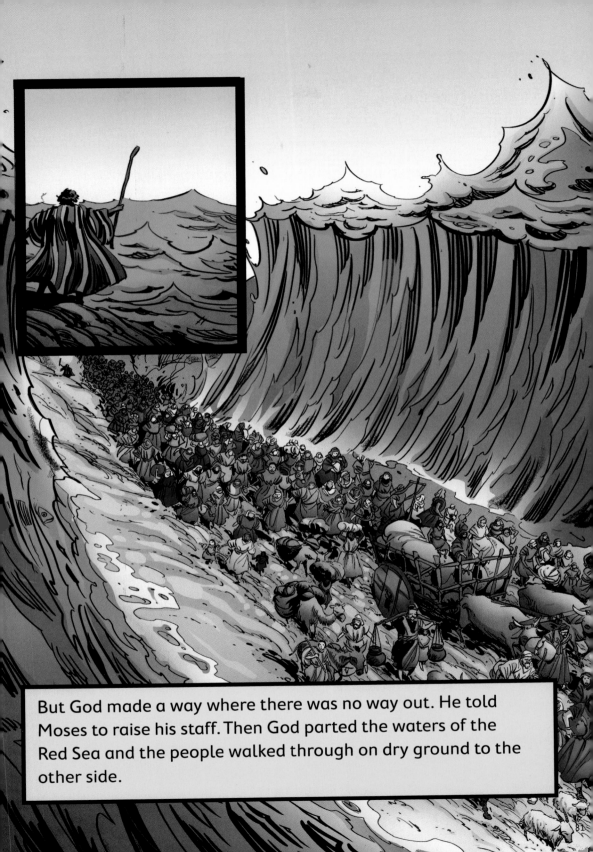

But God made a way where there was no way out. He told Moses to raise his staff. Then God parted the waters of the Red Sea and the people walked through on dry ground to the other side.

Pharaoh and his army tried to follow them, but it was no use—the water crashed down on the Egyptians. God had rescued His people!

They thanked God for saving them. Moses' sister Miriam and other women began to praise God and play tambourines to celebrate.

God took His people through the desert to a new home, called the Promised Land. Every day, God gave them food and water in the desert. And God's people learned to trust Him.

It took a long, long time ... not ten years or twenty years, but forty years before God's people were ready to enter the Promised Land.

God gave them rules to follow; they are called the Ten Commandments. They are God's rules for His people to live in a way that honors Him.

Moses was getting very old. His time as the leader was coming to an end. Who would lead God's people next?

Life, Faith, Action!

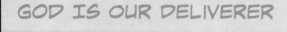

GOD IS OUR DELIVERER

GOD IN ACTION
God hears His people. He knows when we are hurting and need His help. Not only did God save baby Moses, but through Moses, God delivered all His people out of Egypt, against all odds, even performing miracles to give them a way out. God always wants what is best for us. He can do anything to deliver us!

FAITH IN ACTION
Think of a time when God delivered you or your family from a bad situation. What happened? Did it seem impossible? How did God help you?

Dear God, you know us each by name and understand what we are going through. You guide us through everything we face. We remember specific times when you helped us as a family and in our own individual lives too. Thank you for delivering us and for always wanting what is best for us. Amen.

INTO THE PROMISED LAND

Based on Joshua and Judges

Joshua was the next leader God chose for His people. After spending forty years wandering in the desert—eating manna (which tasted like sweetened flat bread) and quail (a type of bird) every single day—God's people were finally ready to enter the Promised Land. They had learned to trust in God and their hearts were focused on Him.

The Jordan River was nearly flooding, but as soon as the feet of the priests touched the water, the river split into two, making a path for God's people to cross … just like the Red Sea had parted forty years earlier. The priests crossed first, carrying the ark of the covenant. It contained the Ten Commandment tablets, Aaron's rod, and a gold pot of manna, the bread from heaven that God gave His people. Then everyone else followed.

Joshua told men from each tribe (there were twelve tribes) to place a stone where God's people had just crossed the river. They used the stones to build a memorial—a reminder to everyone that the One True God keeps His promises.

"Be strong and courageous!" God told Joshua. "I will give you this land, starting with this city Jericho."

God gave Joshua clear instructions for battle: to walk ... walk around the city, carrying the ark of the covenant, for seven days. Then have the priests blow their horns. But before they began, a figure like an angel appeared in front of Joshua with his sword drawn. Joshua asked, "Are you for us or against us?"

The figure replied, "Neither. But as commander of the Lord's army I have now come." Joshua fell facedown to the ground.

After all the people followed God's instructions, the walls of Jericho came tumbling down. Only one person named Rahab and her family escaped. God spared her because she had hidden Joshua's spies before the attack.

After Jericho, Joshua led God's people in a number of battles against other kingdoms in the Promised Land. God gave them victory after victory. He even made the sun stand still during one of the battles, at the city of Ai, because Joshua and his men needed more time (and daylight) to win.

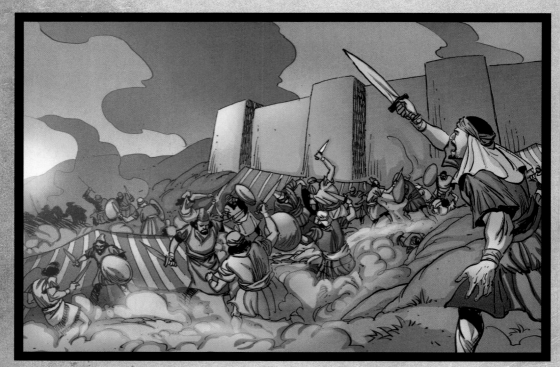

Joshua got older. Before he died, he divided the lands and gave each of the twelve tribes their own kingdoms. Joshua urged them to stay close to God in their hearts. He asked them, "Whom will you serve?" Then Joshua said, "As for me and my household, we will serve the LORD" (Joshua 24:15).

After Joshua died, God sent judges to lead His people in the Promised Land. Othniel, Ehud, Deborah, and others—both men and women—led God's people during this time.

God continued to be with His people, now called the Israelites. When they followed Him, He blessed them. They had plenty of food to eat and grew into a great nation.

Yet they needed many reminders about staying true to God's commands, and not sinning by picking up bad habits from the people they conquered, such as worshiping idols.

Samson was an important judge. He was a Nazirite (someone who doesn't cut his hair or drink alcohol). And he was amazingly strong.

He ripped a city gate from its hinges and carried it over his head. He killed 1,000 enemy soldiers with a donkey's jawbone. With God on his side, no one could stand up to his strength or his power.

His enemies wanted to know the secret of his strength. They offered to pay a woman named Delilah if she could discover his secret.

At first he gave her riddles, and she tried to guess night after night, until finally he told her. While he was sleeping, Delilah had Samson's head shaved; he lost all his strength. Then his enemies gave Delilah her reward money, blinded Samson (who was now powerless), and made him a slave.

But Samson asked God for another chance. "Give me strength one more time so that all people will know you are the One True God. I want to bring you all the honor and glory!"

The Philistine enemies had gathered inside their temple to worship their false god. They chained Samson to two pillars.

God's anger burned against the Philistines, and He granted Samson's request.

Samson pushed apart the pillars and killed all the Philistines when their temple crashed down on them. Samson killed more Philistines on that day than in all his other days combined.

Sadly, God's people drifted away from Him both in their hearts and in their choices. Evil desires and sin—including idol worship—began to rule them.

They also started marrying people who didn't believe in the One True God. God's people forgot about all the blessings God had given them.

The Bible says, "In those days Israel had no king; everyone did as they saw fit" (Judges 17:6). But that would soon change ...

Life, Faith, Action!

GOD LEADS US

GOD IN ACTION

Even though we don't always take time to remember God, He always remembers us. God puts leaders in our lives, as He did in the Bible with the judges, who guide us according to His will. But even if we have leaders, it's still up to us to choose whether or not we will follow.

FAITH IN ACTION

Think about a time when you felt God's presence with you as a family. Did you sense that He was leading you in a specific way? Did other leaders come into your life and help lead you as well? Or was there a time that you decided not to follow God's leading but wish you had? Even when we choose not to follow Him, God still loves us. He is just waiting for us to remember Him and return to Him.

Dear God, please forgive us when we wander away from you, as the people did during the time of the judges in the Bible. Help us see the leaders you've placed in our lives who will guide our choices and bring honor to you. Thank you for always being with us, and for never giving up on us. Amen.

A TIME OF KINGS

Based on 1 and 2 Samuel and 1 and 2 Kings

God's people were getting restless. They didn't want God to lead them through the judges. They wanted a king to rule them, to be like the other countries around them. God warned them through the prophet Samuel that having a king would mean big changes. Their sons would be forced to serve the king, even if it meant going to war, and they would need to give money and supplies to the king (taxes).

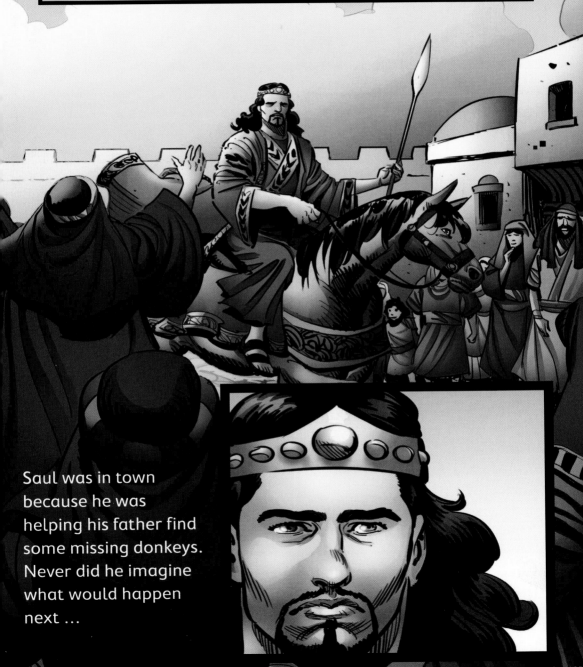

But the people didn't care what it would cost them or what sacrifices it would take. They had their eyes on a man named Saul. He looked the part—strong, tall, and handsome. And he came from a rich and powerful family.

Saul was in town because he was helping his father find some missing donkeys. Never did he imagine what would happen next …

Samuel interviewed Saul and told him he would be the king!

Cheers and shouts went up from the crowd. "Long live the king, long live the king," you can imagine them chanting.

As was the custom in Bible times, leaders were anointed with oil. Samuel took a jar of oil and poured it over Saul's head. This was a sign that God had chosen Saul to be king … the very first king of Israel.

But the people had misjudged King Saul. Inside his heart, he had doubts about himself. And he got jealous easily. The longer he was king, the more unstable he became. Nothing seemed to help.

Meanwhile, out in a field nearby was a young man named David. He was playing his harp and singing to God as he watched over his father's flock of sheep.

God had a plan. He told Samuel to go to a certain shepherd's house and meet his sons. God said to Samuel, "I will let you know whom I choose to be the next king from this family."

Samuel met seven of Jesse's sons but God did not choose any of them.

"Are these all of your sons?" asked Samuel, still waiting for God's voice. "Well," said the father, "my youngest son is out in the field watching the sheep. Surely it's not ..."

... David?"

"Yes, that's the one," said God clearly to Samuel when he saw David.

WHOOSH

It wasn't long before David showed everyone what a perfect choice he was to be the next king. God looks inside at the heart, not at the outside. And David's heart was true to the Lord—even when he was young.

David defeated Goliath in battle with just one stone from a sling. David shouted, "You come against me with sword and spear and javelin, but I come against you in the name of the LORD Almighty ... This day the LORD will deliver you into my hands, and I'll strike you down ..." (1 Samuel 17:45–46).

MUHAHAHAHA!

On his first try, David hit the nine-foot tall giant on the forehead with his stone and he fell down to the ground.

David became an amazing king. He led God's people into battle against other countries that did not believe in the One True God. David conquered many lands and expanded his kingdom. He was a mighty warrior and a great leader. He put his trust in the Lord and not in himself. David was a man after God's own heart.

But David wasn't perfect.
He made some terrible mistakes.
He broke a person's trust.
He had someone killed.
He tried to cover it up.

But there was still hope for David. God blessed him with a son named Solomon, who became the next king. God told Solomon to ask Him for whatever he wanted and Solomon said, "Make me wise." And so God did. In fact, Solomon was the wisest person who ever lived!

God told King Solomon to build a temple. It was magnificent. It took seven years to build and gleamed with gold and jewels. Solomon also built an amazing palace to live in. People came from all over the world to see it and to see King Solomon.

After the great King David and wise King Solomon came dozens and dozens of other kings. Some were good but most were bad. God was not pleased with His people. They kept wandering further and further away from Him in their hearts.

Sometimes God's people would ask for forgiveness and return to the ways God had taught them.

But most of the time they did evil. They worshiped idols. They forgot God's laws. God warned them and urged them to change their ways. But they would not listen. God knew it was time to get His people back on track. But it would mean that they would lose everything. It would mean that once again they would become slaves ... captured by their enemies and taken away into exile—forced to live far from home.

Life, Faith, Action!

GOD IS OUR KING

GOD IN ACTION

In Bible times God's people wanted a human king so they could be like the nonbelievers who lived nearby. But the problem with these kings was that they were not perfect. It was impossible. Only God is our perfect King, the ultimate ruler of our lives. We can always trust Him to rule perfectly over us and His kingdom.

FAITH IN ACTION

Share with each other what comes to mind when you think of the word *king*. How about words like *wise* or *strong* or *handsome*? What is the role of a king? How does a human king compare to our ultimate King? What is the most important quality of being a king?

Dear God, you are our King! Thank you for ruling over us in your perfect way. You always know what is best for us. May we put you at the center of our lives. Help us to trust in you and to do wonderful things for your kingdom. Amen.

A TIME OF EXILE

Based on Esther and Daniel

God's people had turned away from Him. They had forgotten everything God had done for them and had broken their covenant promise with God from the time of Abraham—that they would be His people and He would be their only God.

God had given His people many chances to turn back to Him and remember. He knew what needed to happen. Assyria was a very strong country. Its soldiers invaded the land where God's people lived. Then Babylon invaded. God's people became exiles in Persia. They were taken away from their homes against their wills.

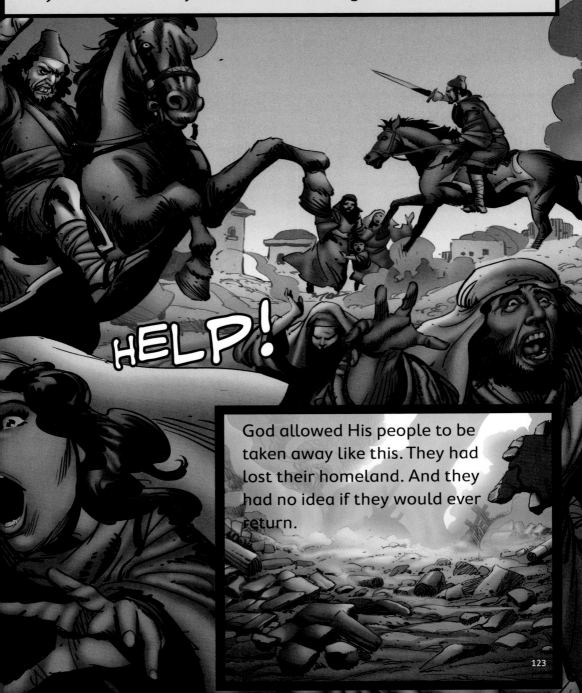

HELP!

God allowed His people to be taken away like this. They had lost their homeland. And they had no idea if they would ever return.

During this dark time for God's people, there lived a young woman named Esther.

She was very, very beautiful. In fact, she won a beauty contest and became Queen of Persia.

But there was trouble. A leader in the king's court was plotting to kill God's people who were in exile. This leader's name was Haman.

PSSST!

Esther's cousin Mordecai encouraged her to try to stop Haman. "And who knows but that you have come to your royal position for such a time as this?" he told her (Esther 4:14).

You see, Esther was one of God's chosen people. She agreed to help ... even though it meant risking her life. "If I perish, I perish," she said (verse 16).

After praying and fasting (not eating anything) for three days, Esther began to put her plan into action. She invited the king to a banquet celebration. And there she told him of the plot to kill God's people, including her. Esther asked for the king's help to save them.

HOORAY!

The king agreed to help. He was so angry about Haman's evil plan that he had Haman hanged.

The people were grateful to the king and queen for helping to save them. God had remembered them!

Also during this dark time of exile, there lived a man named Daniel. He had been taken away from his home in Jerusalem when he was a young man. In Babylon, he and his friends lived among people who did not believe in the One True God. They were ordered to bow down to a statue (an idol) like everyone else. But they refused.

Daniel wasn't there that day, but his friends were punished for not bowing down to the idol. They faced certain death in a fiery furnace ... but God did a miracle. He protected Daniel's friends from the fire. Not one of them was burned!

Daniel's friends stood up for their belief in God. And so did Daniel. He became an important leader in the king's court. Every single day he prayed to the One True God.

The other leaders were jealous of Daniel because King Darius liked Daniel the best. And so they came up with a nasty plan.

The other leaders decided to make a law that all the people in the kingdom would only be allowed to pray to the king.

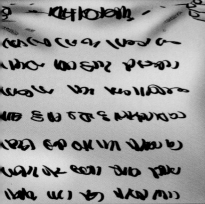

The leaders told the king about their idea for the new law. They talked about how wonderful it would be—such an honor—to have the king's whole kingdom praying only to him. The king couldn't resist. He signed the law.

Daniel heard about the new law, but that didn't change anything for him. Now the leaders had Daniel exactly where they wanted him. It wasn't long before they caught Daniel praying to the One True God. The leaders snatched Daniel and brought him before the king.

The king realized he had been tricked. As much as he liked Daniel, he had to obey the law he had just signed.

"May your God save you," the king said to Daniel as he was taken away to be thrown to the lions.

The king could not sleep all night. He kept worrying about Daniel. He walked back and forth, back and forth, and it felt like the night would last forever. As soon as the sun came up, the king raced to the den. "Daniel!" he called. "Did your God save you from the lions?"

"Yes, my King! God shut the lions' mouths, and I am not hurt at all!"

The king ordered his men to pull Daniel out of the den right away. And he got rid of the other leaders by throwing them into it. They didn't last long down there in the den. Then the king knew what he needed to do: he made a new law that everyone worship the One True God!

Life, Faith, Action!

GOD IS ALL-KNOWING

GOD IN ACTION

Even though God's people were taken into exile and faced danger almost every day, God knew about it all. He was showing them what happens when they don't follow Him and wander away into other religions and beliefs. But God worked through people like Esther and Daniel and his friends to show the power of the One True God. God knew exactly how to keep Esther and His people safe. He also protected Daniel's friends from harm in the fire and Daniel himself when he was face-to-face with the lions. When you are in a hard situation, remember that God is all-knowing and will take you through it to the other side.

FAITH IN ACTION

We can take comfort that God is all-knowing. When we face hard times, God is there with us, giving us exactly what we need. Share a time when you felt that God led you or your family through a way only He knew, but when you look back on it, was perfectly clear.

Dear God, you know everything! You know what we face and you work through our situations and take us to the other side. Help us to always rely on you because your ways are best. Amen.

A TIME OF PROPHETS

Based on Jonah, Daniel, Jeremiah,
Ezekiel, Nehemiah, and Isaiah

During this very hard time in the history of God's people, God did not give up on His promise to them. Even though they had lost their way, and some had even forgotten about God, there was still hope. God wanted His people to remember Him, to ask Him for forgiveness, and to turn from their evil ways.

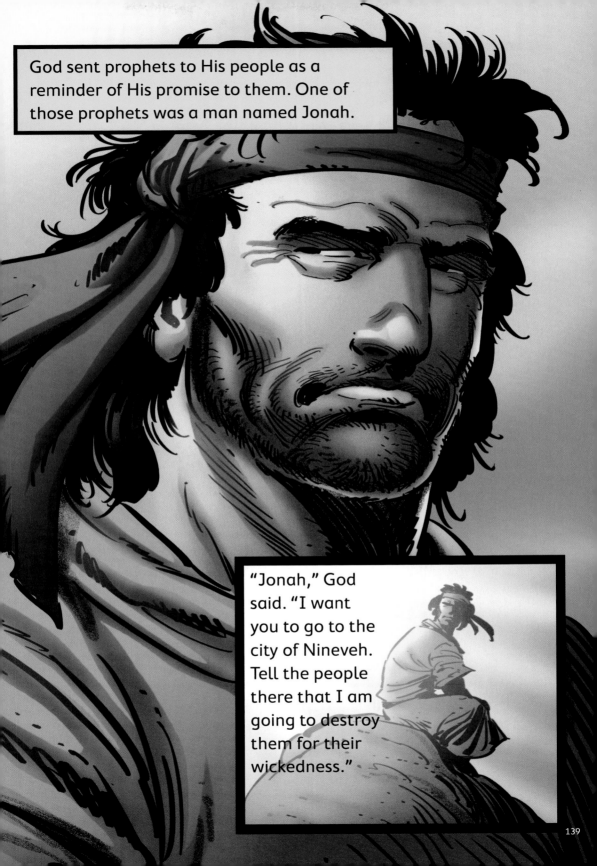

God sent prophets to His people as a reminder of His promise to them. One of those prophets was a man named Jonah.

"Jonah," God said. "I want you to go to the city of Nineveh. Tell the people there that I am going to destroy them for their wickedness."

When God talks to a person and tells him to do something, don't you think he would go ahead and do it? Not Jonah!

In fact, Jonah went in the opposite direction God told him to go. He couldn't believe God wanted him to waste his time on such an evil and horrible group of people in Nineveh. Jonah didn't want anything to do with it ... or them. He looked for a way out and headed for some ships in the distance.

"Do you have room for a passenger?" Jonah called out to a man on one of the boats.

"Yes," answered the man. "We are headed to Tarshish. How about you?"

Jonah snickered to himself and replied, "Perfect. That's perfect." And then he added under his breath, "The opposite direction from Nineveh."

Little did he know what they were in for …

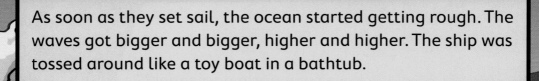

As soon as they set sail, the ocean started getting rough. The waves got bigger and bigger, higher and higher. The ship was tossed around like a toy boat in a bathtub.

"Okay, it's my fault!" confessed Jonah as he yelled over the roaring waves. "I didn't do what God told me to do. Just throw me overboard and then the rest of you will survive this storm."

Sure enough, as soon as they threw Jonah overboard, the sea calmed down. Something else was lurking in the water ... it swam closer and closer toward Jonah. Before he had time to think or scream, Jonah felt the great fish open its mouth and swallow him whole! For three days Jonah prayed to God. "I'm sorry I didn't listen. Please rescue me, Lord, and I will go where you want me to go. I will do what you want me to do."

Jonah screamed as he shot out of the fish's mouth. Can you guess where he landed? Yes! In Nineveh.

When the people of Nineveh heard Jonah's message from God, they realized how sinful they had become. They wanted to leave behind their evil ways and remember God again.

People of all ages and roles in life—young kids, teenagers, moms, dads, grandparents, soldiers, even the king of Nineveh— all humbled themselves before mighty God and asked for forgiveness, for another chance. And God forgave them.

Even though Jonah was also given a second chance, he was having a hard time again with God's plans. He must have thought something like this: *These Ninevites have done so many terrible things, God. Why would you choose to forgive them?*

Unfortunately, Jonah still hadn't learned how to completely obey God, especially when it didn't make sense or was very hard.

God used other prophets, not just Jonah, to bring His messages to His people.

Have you heard the names Jeremiah, Ezekiel, and Isaiah? The Bible talks about sixteen prophets who, over a period of about 350 years, helped bring God's message to His people.

Jeremiah was a young prophet. God's message for His people warned about the doom that was sure to come because they weren't following God's ways. They were worshiping idols instead of God. Jeremiah wasn't very popular and even had to go into hiding for fear he would be killed! But Jeremiah obeyed and was faithful. Unfortunately, God's people didn't listen to Him very well at all.

Ezekiel was another prophet. God promised to restore His people and He used the image of a valley of dry bones to make His point. In a dream God gave Ezekiel, he watched skeletons joining up with muscles and skin to raise a mighty army! "Just trust me," said God. And Ezekiel did.

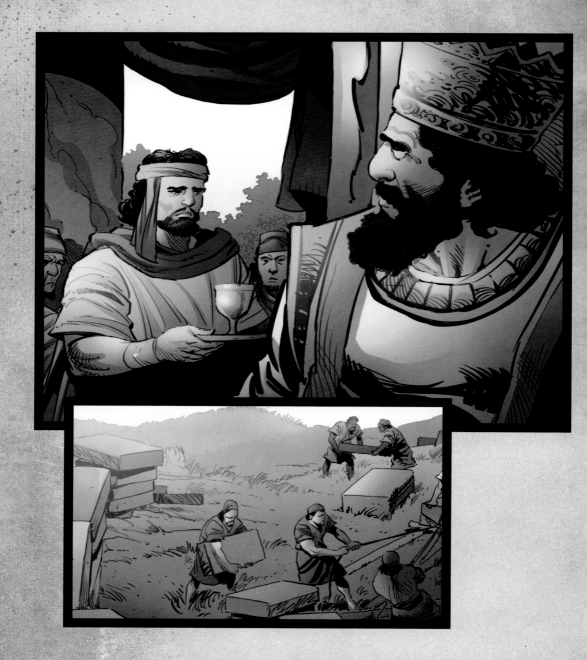

Nehemiah was an important person to know about as well. He was so brave! He prayed for several days before asking the king to let him return to Jerusalem and rebuild the wall that protected the city from its enemies. Not only did they get to go back and rebuild the wall, but God's people also rebuilt their lives with God.

But as much as the prophets told God's people about turning back to Him, God knew it would be impossible unless ...

... God sent Someone to rescue His people from sin once and for all. Isaiah the prophet told about the coming of the Messiah—Wonderful Counselor, Mighty God. Do you know who Isaiah was talking about? Read on!

Life, Faith, Action!

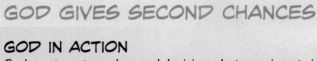

GOD IN ACTION

God wants us to make good decisions, but our sin gets in the way of us being perfect. God is gracious and forgiving. Even though we don't deserve it, He gives us second chances. Sometimes we are confused about why God does, especially with people who make bad choices. But He knows what is best, not us! Soon God would give everyone the ultimate second chance through His very own Son, Jesus.

FAITH IN ACTION

Think of a time when you gave someone in your family a second chance. Share what you remember about it. When were you given a second chance? It goes both ways, doesn't it?

Dear God, we are so thankful that you give second chances. As much as we try to do the right things and make good decisions, we often fall short of your plan for us. Please forgive us, Lord. And help us extend forgiveness to others in order to give them a second chance to make things right. After all, we can't truly accept your gift of second chances if we don't extend it to others. Amen.

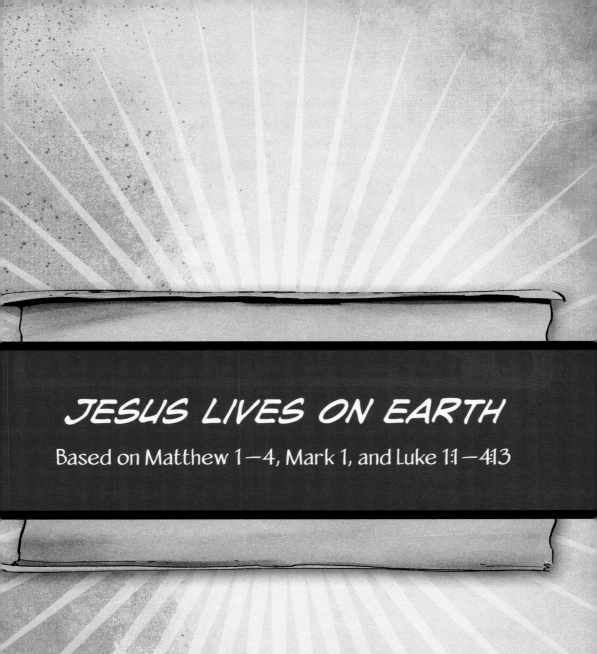

JESUS LIVES ON EARTH

Based on Matthew 1—4, Mark 1, and Luke 1:1—4:13

After God had been silent for hundreds of years, He sent an angel to earth with a very important message. "Mary! You will give birth to a baby boy. His name is Jesus. He is God's Son."

Mary stared at the angel. "How can this be?" But it was true. The angel told Joseph about it too. Several months later, Mary and Joseph had to travel to Bethlehem. It was time for a census, when people returned to their hometowns to be counted.

The only place they found to stay was a simple shelter for animals.
It was also time for Jesus to be born!

Joseph helped Mary as much as he could. And soon they heard a newborn baby's cry. Mary hugged Jesus close.

Nearby, shepherds were watching their sheep in the fields. Suddenly an angel appeared to them.

"Do not be afraid!" said the angel. "I bring you good news of great joy! Today in the town of David a Savior has been born to you; He is Christ the Lord."

Suddenly the nighttime sky was filled with angels singing, "Glory to God in the highest!" The shepherds went to see baby Jesus that very night.

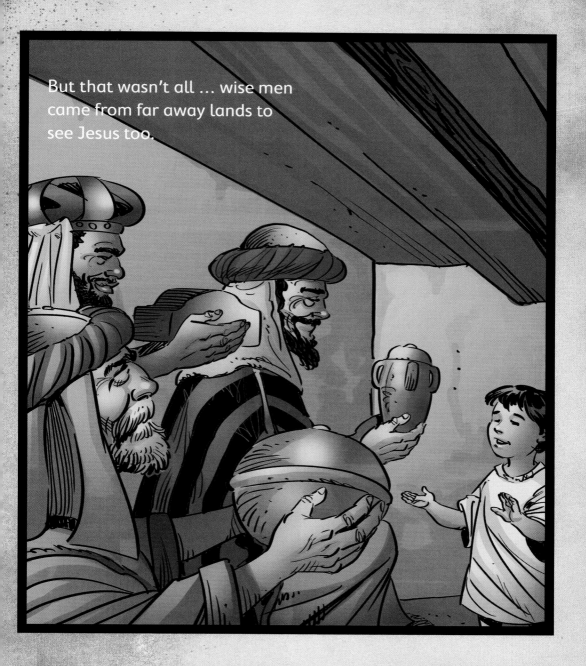

But that wasn't all … wise men came from far away lands to see Jesus too.

It took them a few years to get to Jesus' home. They followed a star that led them to where Jesus lived. The wise men brought Jesus presents—gold, frankincense, and myrrh. These gifts were fit for a king.

Every year during His childhood, Jesus traveled with Mary and Joseph to Jerusalem to celebrate the Passover feast (when God's people remembered their escape from slavery in Egypt and how God had spared the lives of their oldest sons on the night of the last and most terrible plague). This year Jesus was twelve years old. And he had a plan of his own …

Jesus went to the temple courts, where religious leaders were gathered. Jesus began talking with them. They were amazed by how much Jesus knew.

In fact, Jesus knew as much
as they did, even with all their
knowledge and training!

Meanwhile, Mary and Joseph realized that Jesus was missing. They searched the whole city for Him. After three days, they finally found Him at the temple. "Why did you do that?" asked Mary, who was very distressed.

Jesus said, "I had to be in my Father's house."

Mary treasured these things in her heart. She remembered what the angel had told her about Jesus. Then they left Jerusalem and went back home to Nazareth.

As Jesus grew older, He learned how to be a carpenter like Joseph. Not only could He build a house, He could build all the furniture to go inside it. It took years of being an apprentice in order to learn these kinds of skills.

As with everything He did, Jesus worked very hard.

BYE!

Years later, Jesus knew it was time to leave. He wasn't going to be a carpenter. He was the Savior of the world!

But first Jesus had something to do. He walked for several days, all the way to the Jordan River to meet up with His cousin, John the Baptist. John was preparing the way for Jesus, the Messiah.

SPLASH

THIS IS MY SON, WHOM I LOVE.

John lived in the desert. He ate locusts and honey, and wore fur and animal skins for clothes!

God had told John to prepare the way for Jesus; he was baptizing people. And guess what? He baptized Jesus too. As soon as Jesus came up from the water, God said, "This is my Son, whom I love."

Jesus went out into the desert for forty days. He needed time to prepare His mind and spirit for what was next. But then Jesus was put to the test. Satan himself tempted Jesus. He knew Jesus was hungry, with no food to eat in over a month. But Jesus said no. The devil offered Jesus power, but Jesus had His own plan for ruling the world; He didn't need any help from the devil. And Jesus didn't need to prove that God would save Him by jumping from a building either.

Every time Jesus was tempted, He used words from the Bible to fight off Satan.

"DO NOT put the Lord your God to the test."

The devil realized it was no use, so he left Jesus. Then angels came and took care of Jesus. Now Jesus was ready to get to work ...

Life, Faith, Action!

JESUS IS GOD'S SON

GOD IN ACTION

At last it was time for Jesus to come to earth. He was born the way all humans are. His mother Mary gave birth to Him, and she and Joseph raised Him. Not only does Jesus understand what it means to be human, He also understands what it means to be God, since He is God's Son.

FAITH IN ACTION

When you celebrate Christmas, you celebrate Jesus' birthday. What are some favorite family memories you have from Christmastime? Consider lighting a candle or clicking on a flashlight and passing it around as you take turns sharing memories of those times together. What is the best Christmas gift ever? Yes, it's Jesus Christ!

Dear Jesus, God's very own Son. Happy Birthday to you! Help us to always put you as the main focus of our Christmas celebration. You came to earth and understand what it means to be human, yet you also are God. We praise your name! Amen.

JESUS DOES MIRACLES

Based on Matthew, Mark, Luke, and John

Jesus was ready to begin His ministry here on earth. One of the first things He did was to call His twelve disciples who would help Him. (For a full list of their names, go to Matthew 10:2–4 or p. 256.) Jesus did many, many miracles from healing the sick to calming a storm and even bringing people back to life. But His number one goal was to tell people the good news of salvation.

The good news of salvation means that Jesus has saved us from our sins, so we can go to heaven after we die and live with Him and other believers forever. Jesus told the people that He is the Son of God. It was the first time they ever heard this. Jesus needed to tell a lot of people, so He started traveling to different places. Here are some of the miracles Jesus did ...

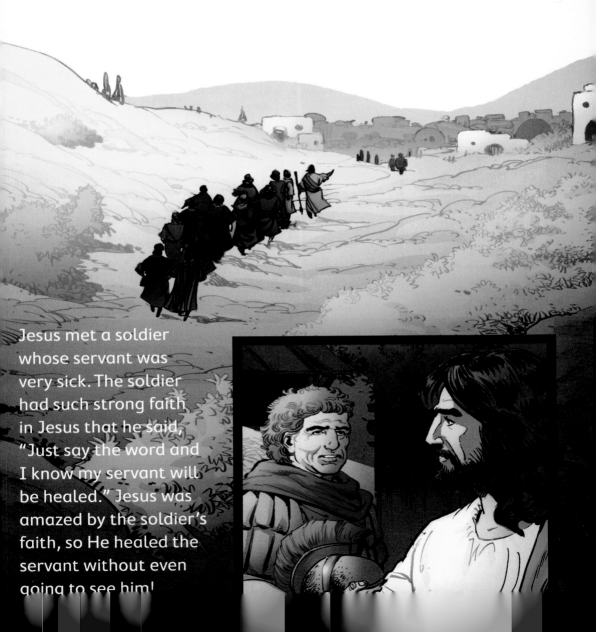

Jesus met a soldier whose servant was very sick. The soldier had such strong faith in Jesus that he said, "Just say the word and I know my servant will be healed." Jesus was amazed by the soldier's faith, so He healed the servant without even going to see him!

One time after Jesus had spoken to a large crowd of people, He and His disciples took a boat to get to the next town.

A huge storm came and although they were tossed around on the water, Jesus was sleeping. The disciples woke Him and said, "Our ship is going to sink! Help us, please help us!"

Jesus stood up and lifted His arm. He said, "Quiet! Be still!" The wind and waves obeyed Him. All at once, the storm stopped. Everyone was amazed by His power!

Jesus visited a town nearby. He went to a little girl's house. A family member had asked Jesus to come because she was very, very sick.

As Jesus was walking to the house, the girl died. "It's too late," her father cried. "My precious girl is gone ..."

But Jesus didn't stop. When He entered the house, Jesus took the girl's hand and said, "Daughter, wake up!" Right away, her eyes opened and she sat up, completely healed. You can imagine how happy and thankful her family was!

Back in Bible times, people with poor vision didn't have glasses to wear. Many who couldn't see very well or were blind couldn't have jobs, so they were often left to beg for their food. It was almost impossible for them to live a normal life. One day, Jesus saw a blind man along the side of the road who was begging for food. Jesus stopped.

Jesus put His hands on the man's eyes. The man blinked a few times, then he looked around and a huge smile spread across his face. He looked into the eyes of Jesus and didn't need to say what he was feeling—Jesus already knew. Not only could the man see, but he could once again lead a normal life. He jumped up and down, praising the Lord.

One time Jesus was teaching a large crowd and it was getting late. The people were hungry. A boy offered his lunch to Jesus. After giving thanks to God for the food, Jesus did a miracle with it and fed over 5,000 people!

Then Jesus went away to be alone for a while. His disciples were on a boat. As they scanned the horizon, they saw a figure out on the water. Who could it be? As the boat got closer, they recognized who it was—Jesus!

The disciple Peter was so excited to see Jesus! He stepped out of the boat onto the water. When he kept his eyes on Jesus, Peter actually walked on water too. But then he looked down, got scared, and started to sink. Jesus reached out to save Peter and brought him back to the boat.

Once Jesus and His disciples were talking about paying money to the ruler at the time; his name was Caesar. Jesus asked Peter to cast out his fishing line and right away Peter caught a fish. It had a coin in its mouth—a miracle! Jesus was showing that God will provide what we need, and we should respect the laws of leaders.

When Jesus was visiting a village near Samaria, He met some outcasts—ten men with a disease called leprosy, which caused horrible and painful sores all over their bodies.

THANK YOU!

Jesus healed all ten of the men. They were amazed and happy and ran into the city to be with their families and friends once again. But they were in such a rush they forgot to thank Jesus. Only one man came back to thank Him. And Jesus was so glad he did!

On another day, one of Jesus' close friends named Lazarus died. One of his sisters came to find Jesus to let Him know. Jesus cried.

Jesus went to where Lazarus was buried. It had been four days since Lazarus had been laid in the tomb. But that didn't stop Jesus. "Lazarus! Come out!" Jesus called (John 11:43). And through the dark opening came Lazarus, his strips of cloth unraveling around him. He was alive again!

Through all the amazing miracles Jesus did while He was here on earth, Jesus wanted to show people that He is the Son of God. And with God, all things are possible! Jesus said, "I am the way and the truth and the life. No one comes to the Father except through me" (John 14:6).

As Jesus continued to travel from place to place, other people followed Him too. They knew Jesus was very, very special. And they would soon understand how deep His love was for them …

Life, Faith, Action!

JESUS IS HEALER

GOD IN ACTION

Jesus has the power to heal us inside and out. He understands how we feel, and He loves us deeply. When Jesus began His ministry on earth, He saw the many sick and hurting people around Him. He not only healed their bodies, He also healed their hearts by explaining that He is their Savior, who could take away their sins and give them eternal life.

FAITH IN ACTION

When you get sick, you can take medicine. It feels so good when you're better, doesn't it? Think about how Jesus is even better than medicine. Not only can He heal your body, He can heal your heart and soul as your Savior. What are some ways you can give thanks to Jesus?

Dear Jesus, our Healer. You can see inside our hearts. And you know exactly how to fix the hurts we have both inside and out. You love us deeply and we love you too. Through your healing, we are able to spend eternal life with you in heaven. Thank you, our precious Savior. Amen.

THE GIFT OF SALVATION

Based on Matthew, Mark, Luke, and John

Jesus loves children. When He was here on earth, Jesus wanted the children to come near to Him. The disciples thought the children were bothering Jesus, but Jesus made sure they knew otherwise. "Let the children come to me," Jesus told the disciples. "Do not keep them away."

Then it was time for a very important week in Jesus' life. It all started on Palm Sunday, when Jesus rode into the city of Jerusalem on a young donkey. This showed that He was a King who was coming in peace and not in war. The people waved palm branches and cheered, "Hosanna!" which is from a Hebrew word that means "save us."

But they didn't understand what was going to happen. They thought Jesus would become their king on earth instead of in heaven.

A few days later, Jesus met with the twelve disciples at a house, in a place called the upper room, for what would be known as the "Last Supper."

Before they sat down to eat, Jesus took a towel and filled a bowl with water. He became like a servant and washed the feet of the disciples. Many of them didn't understand. But Jesus was showing them how to love and serve each other, and that no one is better than anyone else; we should serve all people.

Jesus and the disciples gathered around the table for supper. Jesus became quiet and began to explain some very important things.

Jesus took some bread and broke it. He said, "This is my body, given for you." Then Jesus took a glass and held it up. He said, "This is my blood, poured out for your forgiveness. Eat and drink this to remember me." The disciples thought they were just eating supper with Jesus. But Jesus was showing them how to have Communion, also known as the Lord's Supper.

Earlier that evening, Jesus had said, "This very night one of you will betray me." The disciples couldn't believe what they were hearing. Why would any of them do such a thing?

"Certainly it isn't me, is it, Jesus?" exclaimed one disciple. And so it went, with everyone wondering who it was. But Jesus knew ...

After supper, Jesus took the disciples with Him to the garden of Gethsemane. He needed to pray for a while. But the disciples didn't stay awake to pray—they all fell asleep. Jesus felt so alone. "Please don't make me go through with this, my Father," Jesus prayed. "But if it is your will, then I will do it." Jesus was so distressed because He knew what was coming next.

A path of lights bobbed up and down in the distance. Soldiers! Just as Jesus had predicted, Judas came back and betrayed Jesus that very night. Judas went up to Jesus and kissed Him on the cheek so the soldiers knew who to arrest. What an awful kiss that was.

The next day, Jesus was brought before a leader named Pontius Pilate, with a large crowd watching. "Crucify Him!" the people shouted.

Pilate gave the people a choice of who to let go: Jesus or Barabbas. Barabbas was a criminal, and Jesus was not. Jesus didn't do anything wrong. Guess who the crowd chose to set free? Jesus was sentenced to die on a cross. He carried His own cross out of town, through jeering crowds, to a place called Golgotha, which means "place of the skull."

"Father, forgive them, for they don't know what they are doing," Jesus prayed. Before Jesus gave up His life, He said to God, His Father, "Into your hands I commit my spirit" (Luke 23:46). And then Jesus died.

The earth rumbled and shook in a big earthquake. The sky turned dark. Lightning struck. "Surely this was the Son of God," said a Roman soldier. No one had ever seen anything like it. Jesus' mother Mary cried and cried. Her son was dead. One of the disciples, John, stayed next to her and comforted her.

For two days Jesus was dead and buried in a tomb. But then on the third day something amazing happened. Jesus came back to life! The stone that had covered the entrance to the grave was rolled away. An angel was sitting on top of it. Friends of Jesus came to the tomb and were shocked. "Where have you taken Him?" a friend named Mary asked the angel.

"He is not here! He has risen!" said the angel with joy.

Mary hurried away. She was going to tell the disciples! She thought she bumped into the gardener …

"Mary," said Jesus.

"Oh, it is you, Jesus!" she gasped as she trembled.

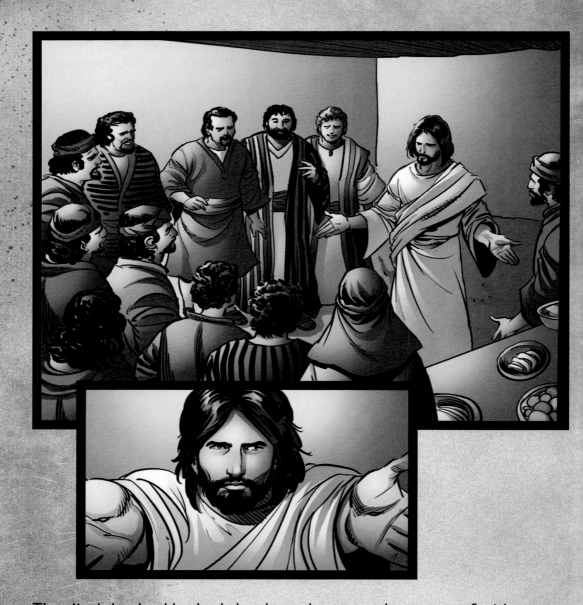

The disciples had locked the doors because they were afraid, but suddenly Jesus appeared in the room with them and said, "Peace be with you." Then Jesus ate some food with them. He explained that He had risen from the dead—Jesus had conquered death! Because of His sacrifice, Jesus had taken away the sins of anyone who believed in Him as their Savior. They would live with Jesus in heaven after they died. The disciples asked Him question after question. They began to realize that Jesus had indeed accomplished what He was sent by His Father to do.

Forty days later it was time for Jesus to leave the earth. He began to rise into the sky back to heaven.

But before He left, Jesus told the disciples and others nearby, "Go and teach others about me, baptizing them in the name of the Father and the Son and the Holy Spirit." This is called the Great Commission. Jesus wants everyone to know about Him as their Savior.

After Jesus left, some angels appeared. They asked, "Why are you looking at the sky like that? Jesus is coming back again someday ... and what a day that will be!"

197

Life, Faith, Action!

GOD IN ACTION

Only Jesus can conquer death and rise again! Hallelujah! He suffered great pain for us. He did this because He loves us so very much. He wants us to be with Him in heaven someday. And this was the only way … to take away our sins and carry them on His shoulders to the cross.

FAITH IN ACTION

Every year during Easter, we remember that Jesus died for us on the cross. And He conquered death by rising from the grave three days later. Jesus is alive! How do you celebrate Easter together as a family? Share something that you are grateful to Jesus for.

Dear Jesus, how can we thank you enough for your sacrifice? You died for us on the cross and then conquered death by rising up from the dead three days later. You gave us the gift of eternal life, the most wonderful gift ever. Jesus, our Savior, thank you! We love you. Amen.

THE CHURCH BEGINS

Based on Acts

After Jesus rose up into heaven on Ascension Day, His disciples
did what He had asked them to do—tell people the good news of
salvation. But first, the people waited for God to give them the
Holy Spirit, which happened on the day we now call Pentecost.
Through the work of the Holy Spirit, the disciples could heal people
who were sick, just like Jesus had done.

The disciples traveled on foot and by boat, telling everyone they could. Do you remember their names? One day Peter and John were walking toward the temple, and a beggar who had been lame from birth asked them for money. Peter said, "Silver or gold I do not have, but what I do have I give you. In the name of Jesus Christ of Nazareth, walk."

Instantly the man's feet and ankles became strong and he could walk again. Soon, more and more people believed in Jesus. And more and more people became disciples of Him!

One of those new followers of Jesus used to be a horrible enemy.

In fact, this man had been responsible for having many believers killed. God decided to use this man in a great and powerful way, but first Jesus would need to change this man's heart.

The man's name was Saul. One day when he was traveling down the road, Saul saw a bright light shining down from heaven.

"Saul! Saul!" called Jesus. "Why are you hurting my people? Why are you persecuting me?" Saul fell to the ground. He was terrified.

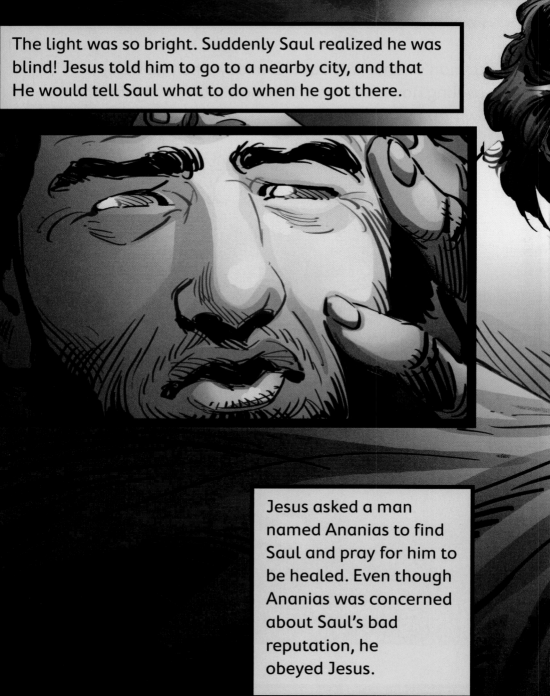

The light was so bright. Suddenly Saul realized he was blind! Jesus told him to go to a nearby city, and that He would tell Saul what to do when he got there.

Jesus asked a man named Ananias to find Saul and pray for him to be healed. Even though Ananias was concerned about Saul's bad reputation, he obeyed Jesus.

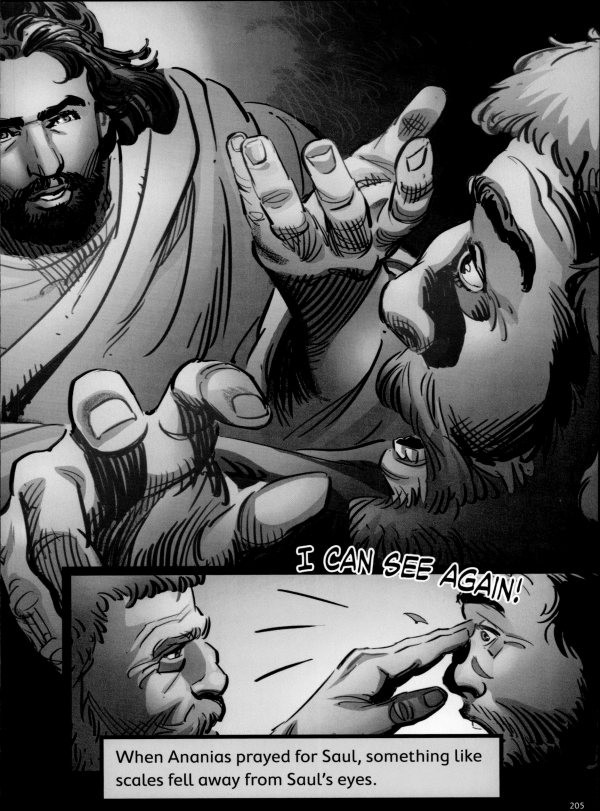

I CAN SEE AGAIN!

When Ananias prayed for Saul, something like scales fell away from Saul's eyes.

Right away Saul's heart was changed. He realized what he had been doing was very wrong. He began his new life as a believer in Jesus. At first the people weren't sure. They still remembered the "old" Saul and all the horrible things he had done.

But it didn't take them long to see that Saul had changed from bad to good. His name had even changed—from Saul to Paul. The people listened to him tell the good news about Jesus.

Paul first told the Jewish people in Rome. He was Jewish too, and had a lot of knowledge and training.

He knew how to explain things about Jesus in ways that helped them understand and believe. He reminded the Jewish leaders how God had told His prophets that Jesus would be the Messiah, and He would be born in a place where animals take shelter. Paul reminded them that Jesus matched all the predictions, or prophecies, from the Bible.

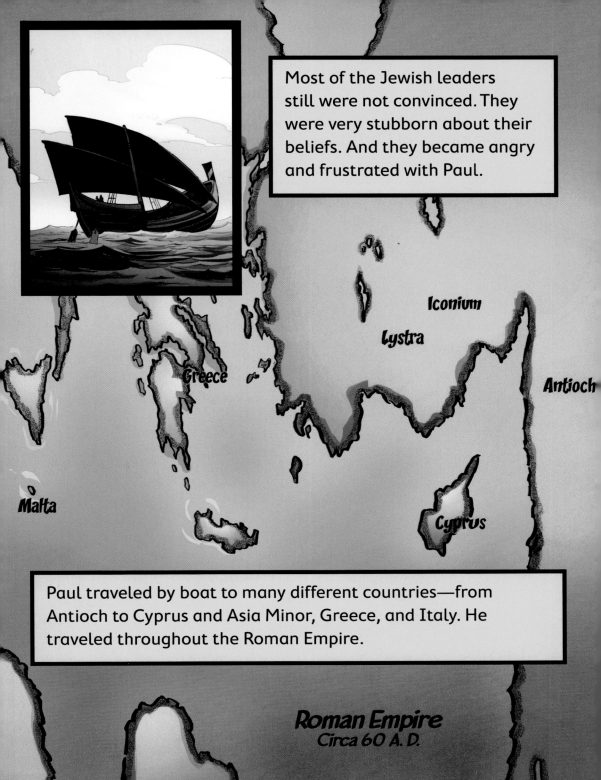

Most of the Jewish leaders still were not convinced. They were very stubborn about their beliefs. And they became angry and frustrated with Paul.

Iconium

Lystra

Greece

Antioch

Malta

Cyprus

Paul traveled by boat to many different countries—from Antioch to Cyprus and Asia Minor, Greece, and Italy. He traveled throughout the Roman Empire.

Roman Empire
Circa 60 A. D.

Paul had friends, like Timothy and Barnabas, who traveled with him. Sometimes they stayed in the cities to help start groups where believers could keep learning about God and support each other as a community of Christians. It's what we call the church.

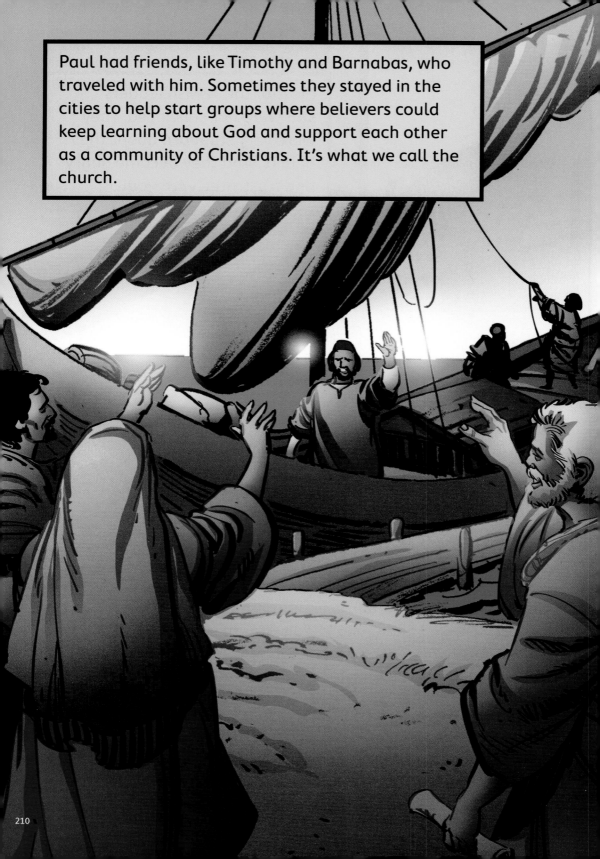

STOP THAT MAN!

Some people tried to stop Paul from spreading the good news. In fact, Paul was put in jail many times. So then instead of traveling to different places, Paul wrote letters. Many of these letters are found in the Bible. They are called the "Epistles (or letters) of Paul."

The Bible has many important things to tell us today. It contains the words of God. Just like the disciples of Jesus and Paul and all their helpers, we can spread the good news of Jesus.

Do you have a friend who doesn't know about Jesus?

You can start by telling your friend about John 3:16 from the Bible: "For God so loved the world that he gave his one and only Son, that whoever believes in him shall not perish but have eternal life."

Life, Faith, Action!

GOD GIVES US GOOD NEWS!

GOD IN ACTION

Jesus gave us the best news ever—the good news of salvation! Through His time here on earth, Jesus showed us how to live, how to love, how to care for one another, even how to pray. But Jesus didn't want things to end with Him when He returned to heaven. That's why He sent His Holy Spirit to be with us when we ask Him. On the day Jesus ascended to heaven, He left us with a job to do—tell others about the good news of salvation for everyone, all around the world.

FAITH IN ACTION

As a family, talk about the Great Commission. Open up the Bible to Matthew 28:19–20 and take turns reading it together. Sharing this good news makes God so very happy! How can you tell others about Jesus?

Dear God, we have the best news to share with others. Please help us find ways to do this. Give us the courage to tell our friends about you. Thank you for the gift of Jesus, who has opened the door to heaven. Amen.

JESUS WILL RETURN

Based on Revelation

Did you know that Jesus is coming back to earth someday? Long ago, on Ascension Day, the angels told the disciples that Jesus would come back the same way He left (see page 197).

At the very end of the Bible, one of Jesus' disciples, named John, wrote down what Jesus said heaven will be like. Jesus' voice sounded like a trumpet. The hair on His head was as white as snow, and His eyes were like blazing fire. John fell at His feet, as though dead, but Jesus said, "Do not be afraid. I am the First and the Last. I am the Living One; I was dead, and now look, I am alive for ever and ever!" (Revelation 1:17–18).

Then Jesus explained, "The seven stars in my right hand are the angels of the seven churches. And the seven lampstands are the seven churches." Did you know that the number seven is a symbol that means "completion"?

Jesus spoke to each of the seven churches and told them what they had been doing right and also how they could have done better.

Jesus was hard on the seven churches but He explained, "Those whom I love I rebuke and discipline. So be earnest and repent. Here I am! I stand at the door and knock. If anyone hears my voice and opens the door, I will come in and eat with that person, and they with me" (Revelation 3:19–20).

Jesus not only encouraged the seven churches to follow Him as their Savior, He also urged them to stand up under the forces of evil and the coming battle.

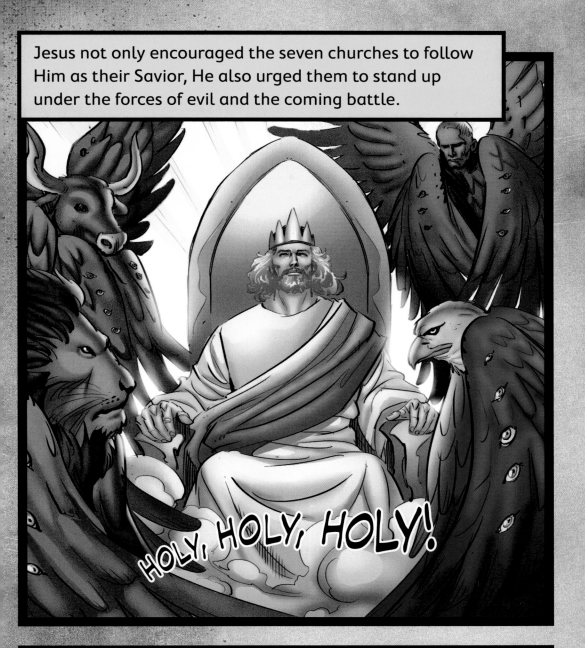

HOLY, HOLY, HOLY!

Jesus showed John what heaven looked like. Rainbows and jewels and dazzling light surrounded them. Four creatures gathered around the throne. They never stopped saying these words, night and day: "'Holy, holy, holy is the Lord God Almighty,' who was, and is, and is to come" (Revelation 4:8).

Jesus told John about many symbols and signs that will happen. It was a foretelling of the end times. We aren't sure exactly what they all mean.

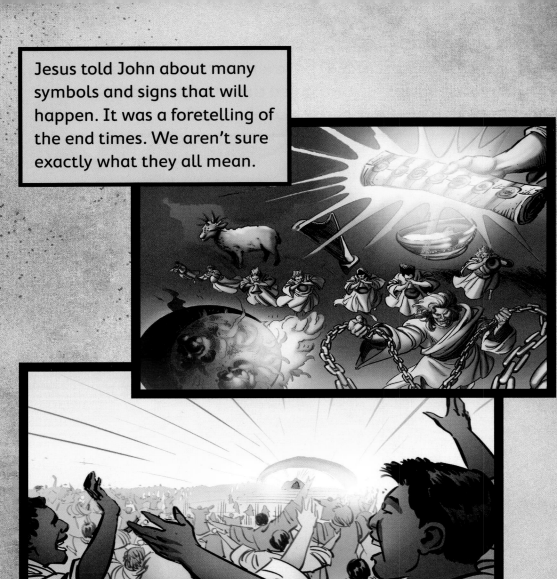

But we do know that when Jesus comes back to earth, He will be riding on a white horse in full glory. His eyes will be like blazing fire, and on His head will be many crowns. "KING OF KINGS AND LORD OF LORDS" will be written on His leg.

When Jesus returns, He will do battle with Satan. And Jesus will win! The devil will be defeated once and for all. The Bible says, "Salvation and glory and power belong to our God" (Revelation 19:1).

And He who is sitting on the throne will say, "Behold, I am making all things new." Then Jesus described the "new Jerusalem." Remember how beautiful the old Jerusalem was, back when David was king, and then his son Solomon? Well, this new city will be amazing. It will be surrounded by God's glory, and all believers inside will enjoy God for eternity—forever!

TO GOD BE THE GLORY

Then Jesus showed John the River of Life that flowed from the throne of God through the middle of the street of the city. There will be no need for lights or the sun, because the Lord God will be the light. Nighttime will be no more.

No one knows the exact date and time when Jesus will return. Only God knows. When that day does come, Jesus will send out His angels with a loud trumpet call. All the nations around the world will see the Son of Man.

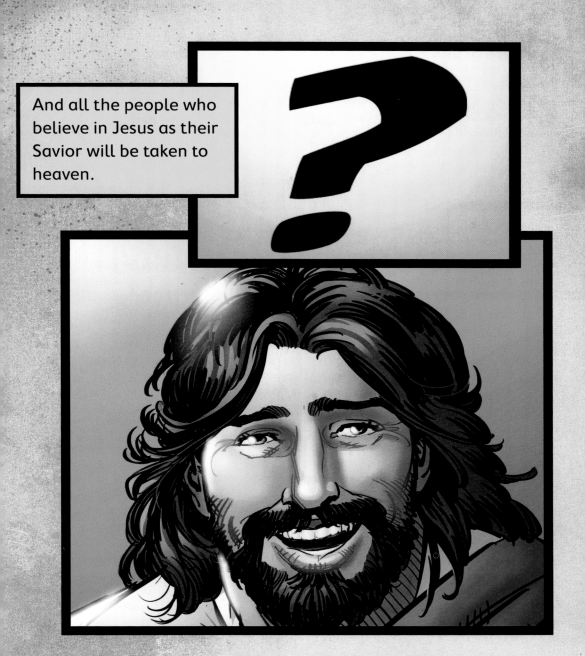

And all the people who believe in Jesus as their Savior will be taken to heaven.

Jesus said, "Yes, I am coming soon." And what an amazing day that will be!

"The grace of the Lord Jesus be with [you]. Amen" (Revelation 22:21).

Life, Faith, Action!

GOD IN ACTION

Jesus will return one day, and what a day that will be! While we don't know exactly when this will happen, and many things about it are a mystery, we do know that Jesus will conquer the devil once and for all. We will no longer sin but will be taken to heaven to live with God and to praise Him forever. There will be no more death or sadness, only joy and happiness … the kind that you never get tired of, the kind that feels like a dream come true.

FAITH IN ACTION

Talk together about what you think heaven will be like. What are you looking forward to? Will you have pain or suffering? Will there be sin in heaven? What are some questions you have about heaven?

Dear Jesus, we know you will come back one day. We look forward to that day! Not only will you defeat Satan once and for all, but you will also take us to heaven to live with you forever. We thank you for this gift of salvation, by suffering and dying on the cross, carrying our sins, and then rising from the dead three days later. You conquered death for us so we can have life forever with you! Amen.

FOR GOD SO LOVES US

Based on the Entire Bible

Throughout time God has been, and is, at work. He knows all things, including your very own name ... even the number of hairs on your head! Ever since God made the world, and the first man and woman (remember their names?), He has been loving and caring for us and His creation.

Even though sin entered the world through people choosing to listen to the devil instead of God, God still loves His people. He established a covenant promise with Abraham that He would be our God and we would be His people. And as God's people grew in number—from Abraham to Isaac and Jacob and beyond—God kept His promise.

But God's people did not keep their part of the promise. Sometimes they followed God and obeyed His commandments, but many other times they wandered away to worship false gods and lived in evil ways.

Through Joseph, God showed His power to Egypt. But Joseph and God's people grew so large in number that the pharaoh became concerned.

And so the pharaoh forced God's people into slavery. God's people cried out to Him, and God heard them. He called on Moses to free His people. Through God's mighty power—including parting the waters of the sea—Moses led God's people to freedom.

But they didn't follow God with their whole hearts. They complained. They still didn't completely put their trust in Him. So they wandered in the desert for forty long years.

Moses died in the desert as an old man, but Joshua led God's people into the Promised Land. He was known as a strong and courageous leader. He said, "As for me and my household, we will serve the LORD" (Joshua 24:15). After entering the Promised Land, Joshua followed God's instructions to march around the city of Jericho and boom! Down came the walls. Whenever they trusted in God, His people had success. But whenever they turned away from Him, they suffered.

God sent judges like Deborah and Samson to lead them. And then God even chose kings like Saul and David and Solomon to lead them. But still, they wandered away from Him.

God knew it was time to make a change. This cycle of sinning and then repenting and then sinning again just wasn't what He wanted for His people. He had a different forever plan.

God sent prophets like Jonah and Isaiah and Jeremiah to tell His people to turn away from their sins. Sometimes they listened, but most of the time they didn't.

So God allowed His people to be captured again as slaves. They lost their beautiful city of Jerusalem along with the beautiful temple and palace Solomon had built when he was king. It was destroyed by enemies who did not believe in God. But still, God did not forget about His people. He still loved and cared for them deeply.

He put Esther in a high position as Queen of Persia. And through her influence, God saved His people once again. Eventually God's people were set free. They were allowed to return to their homeland and rebuild Jerusalem and the temple and the walls surrounding the city.

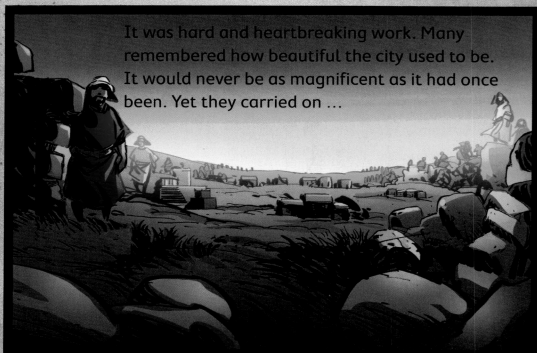

It was hard and heartbreaking work. Many remembered how beautiful the city used to be. It would never be as magnificent as it had once been. Yet they carried on ...

God was silent for a long, long time ... for hundreds of years.

Until it was time for the Savior to come. His name is Jesus, God's very own Son.

I LOVE YOU.

He was born in a simple shelter, next to sheep and cows and chickens. Angels announced His birth to shepherds in fields nearby. They filled the sky with singing! "Glory in the highest, and on earth, peace among men."

The shepherds left their sheep and went to see Jesus. They told people along the way about it too. Soon after, wise men from the east also came to see Jesus. They brought Him presents of gold, expensive spices, and perfume—all gifts fit for a king.

It wasn't long before Jesus was ready to start His ministry. He was baptized in the Jordan River by His cousin, John the Baptist. Remember him? John wore rugged clothes and ate locusts and honey out in the wilderness. God had told John to prepare the way for Jesus, to tell the people to be baptized.

Jesus called twelve disciples to help Him with His ministry. These men went with Jesus by foot and by boat. They saw Jesus doing amazing things: healing the sick, feeding people, calming the sea, walking on water, and raising the dead. People began talking about Jesus, and the good news about Him spread.

Some leaders did not agree that Jesus was the Savior. And they gave Jesus a hard time. In fact, they paid one of the disciples to betray Jesus.

IT IS FINISHED

While Jesus was eating His last supper with them, Judas ran out the door. Afterward, Jesus went to a garden to pray. He knew the time was soon coming when He would give His life to save people from their sins. He asked God if there was any other way than to give His life, but He would obey, if that was His Father's will. And it was.

Judas showed up that same night with Roman soldiers. Just one day later, Jesus hung on the cross, tried as a criminal, when He had done nothing wrong. Praise be to God, the best part of God's story is that this wasn't the way it would end.

In fact, it's really just the beginning!

Yes, Jesus died on the cross, but three days later He rose from the dead! He conquered death to save us from our sins. And before He went back up to heaven, Jesus told the disciples to let the world know that He is the Savior of all people.

So the disciples did! And then people like Paul joined in telling others about the good news of Jesus.

Iconium

Lystra

Antioch

Greece

Malta

Cyprus

This good news kept spreading around the world. And soon churches were started, where people could gather and praise God together and encourage each other in their faith. People kept sharing with others the good news of Jesus. And they still do today.

Life, Faith, Action!

GOD IN ACTION

At the center of everything God does is His love. As we've seen throughout this book, from creating a beautiful world to leading through hard times, from keeping His promises to delivering from danger, from healing to saving, we know how to love because God first loved us.

FAITH IN ACTION

Talk as a family about God's love. How do you feel His love? Share times when you have felt His love. Parents, try to describe how much you love your children. Now, together think about how much more God loves you, even more than your parents!

Dear God, from the beginning of time you have loved us. You created us in your very own image. And you made a beautiful world for us to live in. When sin came into our lives, you gave us the gift of salvation through your Son, Jesus Christ. Thank you for coming to earth to live with us, for understanding completely what we experience, both good and bad. May we show love to others in a way that reflects your love, so they may also experience your everlasting love. Amen.

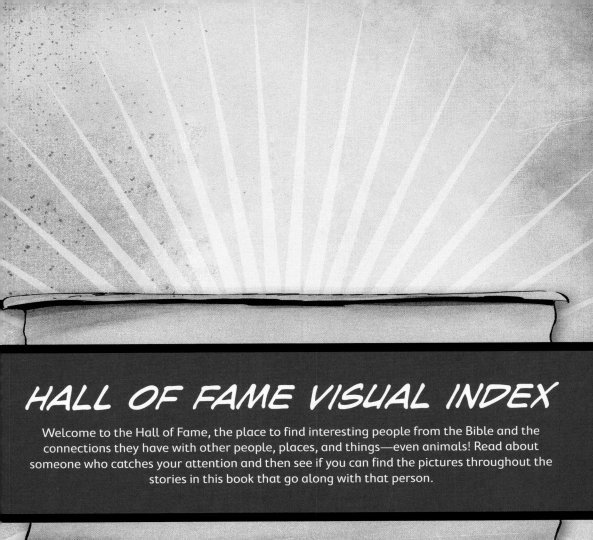

HALL OF FAME VISUAL INDEX

Welcome to the Hall of Fame, the place to find interesting people from the Bible and the connections they have with other people, places, and things—even animals! Read about someone who catches your attention and then see if you can find the pictures throughout the stories in this book that go along with that person.

ACTIVE HEALER WONDERFUL PERFECT
CREATOR PATIENT ETERNAL GENTLE
MESSIAH GOOD SAVIOR
RESURRECTED

JESUS

First let's talk about the most amazing Hero who ever lived—Jesus! See how many words you can find that describe Jesus. What other words can you think of that tell about Him?

FORGIVING VICTORIOUS
COUNSELOR
TRUSTWORTHY
CRUCIFIED
REMARKABLE
COMPASSIONATE
RIGHTEOUS
LOVING
CHRIST
DELIVERER
PURE
SUFFERED
SAFE
HOLY
POWERFUL
ALIVE
AMAZING
PRINCE OF PEACE
ALMIGHTY GOD MIGHTY

JESUS

PAGES 151–200, 237–246

God's one and only Son came to earth and was born, grew up to be a man, and fulfilled His mission to be the Savior of the world. Jesus proved His power to conquer death, not only for Himself but also for all people who believe in Him. Someday Jesus will return; He will destroy Satan and take all Christians to heaven to live forever with Him. Check out all the connections Jesus has ... with everyone!

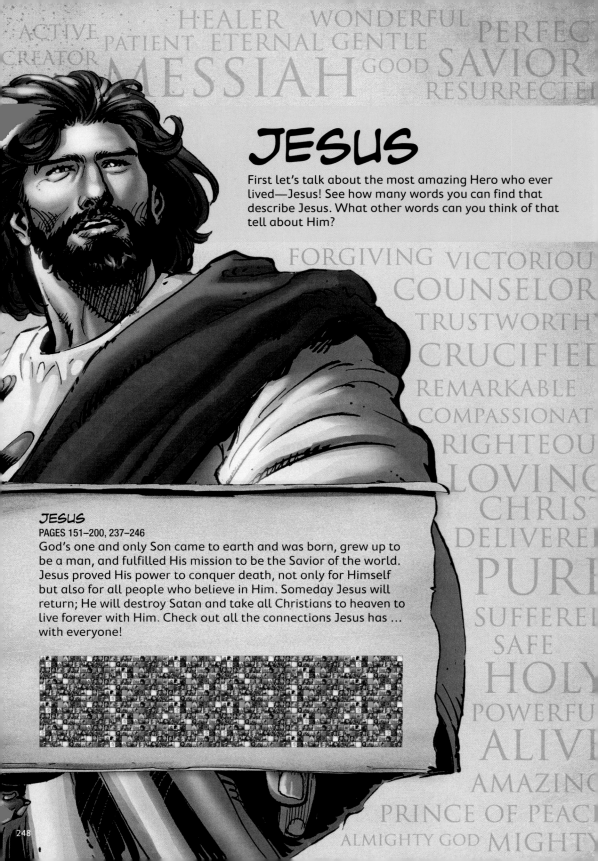

Hall of Fame Visual Index

AARON

Brother to Moses and Miriam, came to Moses' side when it was time to tell Pharaoh to let God's people go! Aaron had a way with words, so he did most of the talking.

ABRAHAM

God called Abraham and made an unbreakable promise with him that would stand the test of time, generation after generation—He would be their God and they would be His people. Here's the thing: Abraham didn't even have any children until he was an old man. That takes a lot of trust in a plan that requires having kids!

ADAM

First man to ever exist, created by God from the dust of the ground. Adam named all the animals and God told him to take good care of the earth. Life was perfect, but then Adam gave in to temptation by eating the forbidden fruit and was cast out of the garden of Eden.

DANIEL

Taken to a land far away with some of his friends and became a trusted advisor to King Darius. When his faith was tested, Daniel stayed true. He prayed only to the One True God, even if it meant having a sleepover with fierce lions. God kept their mouths shut so Daniel was safe.

DEBORAH

When other leaders showed fear in the face of battle, Deborah was out in front, leading the way. She was one tough judge! She is a good reminder to us that we can all be heroes for God. It just requires trusting in Him.

Hall of Fame Visual Index

ESTHER

A young maiden who won a beauty contest and became queen suddenly found herself at the center of an earth-shattering, life-threatening event in history. By asking for help from God and her king, she undid Haman's plot to kill God's people ... including her.

PAGES 124–127, 136, 235

EVE

First woman to ever exist, created by God from one of Adam's ribs. She and Adam took care of all the animals and she was the very first mother. Life was perfect until she was tricked by a serpent (Satan, the devil). Eve gave in to temptation by eating the forbidden fruit and was cast out of the garden of Eden.

PAGES 13–25

EZEKIEL

This prophet of God saw some amazing things including glimpses into heaven, edible scrolls and coals, and even a valley of dry bones coming to life again as an army of God. Ezekiel was used by God in mighty ways; he told God's people what was going to happen in the future.

PAGES 148–149

ISAAC

Boy, were Isaac's parents glad to see him! They had waited decades for him to be born because he was the key to God's unbreakable promise with his father, Abraham. When Sarah passed away, Abraham sent for a wife for Isaac. Her name was Rebekah. And it was love at first sight. Really.

PAGES 44–54, 229

ISAIAH

This prophet of God told about the coming of Jesus—the Messiah, King of Kings and Lord of Lords. His words would come true—not that day or the next day, but 400 years later.

PAGES 148, 151, 233

Hall of Fame Visual Index

JACOB

Shepherd and father to Joseph and eleven other sons. He gave Joseph a beautiful coat and was later deceived that a wild animal had put an end to Joseph. Eventually father and son—and all the sons—were reunited in Egypt.

PAGES 56–62, 69, 229

JEREMIAH

This prophet of God had a hard time getting people to take him seriously. Once he went into the king's palace wearing an oxen yoke. And he was sent down into a well for several days. His news felt too much like "doom and gloom" and people just didn't want to hear it. But they should have listened …

PAGES 148, 233

JOHN

This disciple of Jesus got to see into the future, to the end times when Jesus will return. John wrote down the vision Jesus gave him, which is written in the book of Revelation. Amazing creatures, Jesus riding a white horse, lampstands, scrolls, and more!

PAGES 170, 184–191, 193–201, 216–225

JOHN THE BAPTIST

This man lived in the wilderness, wore animal skins for clothes, and ate honey and … locusts for lunch. God gave him an important job—to prepare the way for Jesus by baptizing people. Did you know John and Jesus were cousins?

PAGES 164–165, 239

JONAH

God told this prophet to go to a sinful city and tell the people to turn from evil. But Jonah went the opposite way. He eventually made it there, by way of a fish, and did what God commanded. He wasn't happy about it, even after God had just saved *him*! He was a confused prophet.

PAGES 139–147, 152

Hall of Fame Visual Index

JOSEPH (OLD TESTAMENT)
Received special treatment from his dad until his jealous brothers threw him into a pit and sold him as a slave. God was always with Joseph. Despite being accused of a crime he didn't commit, spending years in jail, and missing his dad, God took care of Joseph. And Pharaoh knew a good advisor when he saw one.

PAGES 57–70, 230

JOSEPH (NEW TESTAMENT)
Mary's future husband was ready to break up when he found out she was pregnant, but an angel stopped him with a message in a dream: "Go ahead with the wedding because the child she carries is from God." Joseph fulfilled the prophecy from the Bible that Jesus would come from the family line of King David.

PAGES 154–163, 168, 237

JOSHUA
This strong and courageous leader took God's people into the Promised Land. Jericho was the one city in the way, but not for long. The walls came tumbling down—not through hand-to-hand combat, weaponry, or physical force, but through obedience … and the sound of blowing rams' horns.

PAGES 88–93, 231

JUDAS
This disciple of Jesus betrayed Jesus for thirty pieces of silver (worth about 600 dollars today). Judas told enemies of Jesus where to find Him. That's why the soldiers came to arrest Jesus and take Him to go on trial just like a criminal. Judas couldn't live with himself after that.

PAGES 170, 184–191, 240–241

KING DARIUS
This friend of Daniel was tricked into signing a law that almost got Daniel killed. Then the king issued another law that his kingdom would pray to God and no other. His palace had a place where bad guys went and never returned … the lions' den. Ever heard of it?

PAGES 130–136

Hall of Fame Visual Index

PAGES 109–120, 222, 232

KING DAVID

Whether a shepherd boy or later a king, this man expressed his love for the Lord in ways that greatly pleased God. David was sincere, and he was mighty in battle. He also had amazing musical and writing talent. He was a true warrior for God. But even he wasn't perfect …

PAGES 104–108, 120

KING SAUL

Israel's first king. Saul looked promising but never lived up to the title. Driven to madness by jealousy, masked with hatred for his successor … King David.

PAGES 116–120, 222

KING SOLOMON

Son of David and heir to the throne. Solomon was given wisdom from the Lord like no other. He spared no expense when he built the glorious temple of the Lord and the palace. But Solomon didn't stay faithful to the One True God.

PAGE 179

LAZARUS

What's it like to die and come back to life? Lazarus knows. His sisters sent a message to Jesus but He didn't come right away. Some say Jesus wanted to show His power over death by bringing Lazarus back to life, a preview of His own resurrection. Can you imagine the wonder Lazarus felt?

PAGES 154–163, 168, 193, 237

MARY

After receiving shocking news, from an *angel*, Mary accepted that she was going to have a baby and that He would be God's Son. Talk about faith! Even to the point of giving birth … in a simple shelter for animals! Every step of the way, Mary was obedient to God. Sounds like a great mother for Jesus.

Hall of Fame Visual Index

PAGES 73–74, 83

MIRIAM
Sister to Moses, Miriam watched over him as a baby, especially when he was on the riverbank of the Nile in a floating basket. She was also at the crossing of the Red Sea, singing and playing the tambourine to celebrate the deliverance of God's people from slavery.

PAGE 125

MORDECAI
Cousin to Esther, he risked his life supporting her as queen and also gave her great advice—even when it meant meeting with her in the middle of the night. He also ended up with an important role in the palace, replacing evil Haman, who had plotted against God's people to destroy them.

PAGES 72–86, 230–231

MOSES
God worked through Moses in mighty ways—from the time he was a baby to his death in the desert. God delivered Moses in a basket, talked to him from a burning bush, divided a sea for safe passage, gave him the Ten Commandments on a mountaintop, and led His people for forty years in the desert.

PAGES 26–38

NOAH
Chosen by God to save all the animals and his family from the great flood. Noah's trust in God and hard work paid off. Carpenter, zoo keeper, ship captain—Noah answered the call. They floated on the ark for over a year. What's the first thing they did when they got off the ark? Thanked God … and kissed the ground.

PAGES 202–214, 243

PAUL
Transformed to a believer after a blinding "come to Jesus" moment that brought him to his knees. He traveled to many countries, by land and by sea, telling people all about Jesus. Even in jail (he didn't do anything wrong), Paul found ways to keep sharing the good news—his letters, known as the Epistles, are in the Bible.

Hall of Fame Visual Index

PETER
This disciple of Jesus actually walked on water, if only for a few seconds. He had his highs and lows but eventually understood who Jesus was. He healed people in Jesus' name and he also gave the big speech on the day of Pentecost, when the Holy Spirit came to live in His believers.

PAGES 170, 176–177, 184–191, 196–198, 200–201

REBEKAH
This young woman seemed to be at the right place at the right time. But it was really God's perfect timing. After passing a simple test of offering water to a servant and his camels, she was chosen to be Isaac's wife. And it was truly love at first sight.

PAGE 52

SAMSON
As long as Samson didn't cut his hair, God kept him strong. But Samson lost everything when he told his girlfriend the secret of his strength; Delilah traded his trust for money. She was the last thing he saw before he was blinded … for life.

PAGES 96–99, 102, 232

SAMUEL
Called by God as a boy (it took him a while to figure out who was talking to him in the middle of the night), Samuel grew up to become Israel's last judge. He anointed the first king. Samuel relayed message after message, trying to make God's will known and followed.

PAGES 104–112

SARAH
Sarah waited most of her life. God promised her and her husband, Abraham, a son who would unlock their future, to be blessed by God generation after generation. She became a mom when she could have been a great-grandma at the age of ninety! Can you blame her for laughing when God told her the news?

PAGES 42–45, 54

Hall of Fame Visual Index

SATAN (ALSO KNOWN AS THE DEVIL)

Worst villain of all time. His name means "adversary" or "one who opposes." Cast out of heaven for wanting to be greater than God. The devil challenges God's plans by lying, tempting, and deceiving. But God fights for His people. When Jesus returns, He will destroy Satan. Satan will spend eternity in the lake of fire (Revelation 20:16).

PAGES 16–21, 166–167, 221, 226

THE TWELVE (ALSO KNOWN AS THE DISCIPLES)

The twelve disciples were men chosen by Jesus for a mission—to tell people about Him as God's Son and Savior. Their names were Andrew, Bartholomew, James, James (the younger), John, Judas, Jude (or Thaddeus), Matthew, Peter, Philip, Simon, and Thomas. Some wrote books of the Bible.

PAGES 170–181, 184–197, 200–201, 217–225, 240–242

YAHWEH (YAH-way)

This name for God means "I Am" in the ancient Hebrew language (of Old Testament times). They felt it was too sacred to be said out loud. It shows that God never had a beginning and never has an end. He is the same yesterday, today, and forever. "Lord" in small capital letters in the Bible was translated from the word *Yahweh*.

PAGES 76–77

YOU!

Did you know you are part of God's story? He has wonderful plans for you. And He will be with you every day, for the rest of your life. If you aren't sure what that means for you, just talk to Him. You could pray something like this: "Dear God, I want to know you more and understand your ways. Please show me. Thank you for always being with me. In Jesus' name. Amen."

May the Lord bless you and keep you. May His face shine upon you and give you peace, both now and always!

(Numbers 6:24-26)